# Jascha Heifetz
Through My Eyes

# Jascha Heifetz
## Through My Eyes

The eyes are the mirror of the soul
*(traditional proverb)*

### Sherry Kloss

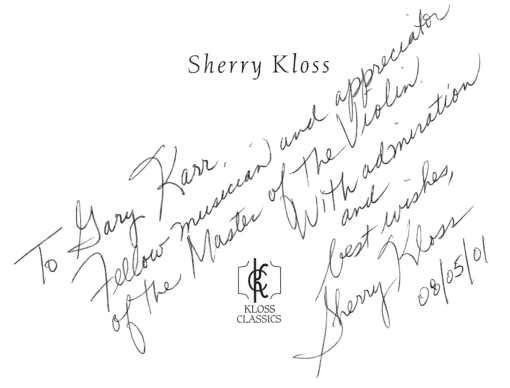

KLOSS
CLASSICS

© 2000 Sherry Kloss. All right reserved.

All rights reserved. No part of this book may be reproduced or transmitted in any form or by any means, electronic or mechanical, including photocopying, recording or by any information storage and retrieval system without written permission from the author, except for the inclusion of brief quotations in a review.

KLOSS CLASSICS
Ball State University/Music
Muncie, Indiana  47306-0220   USA

Book cover and interior design by Lightbourne

Cover photo credits: Jascha Heifetz, BMG Classics
                    Sherry Kloss, Soheil Navidbakhsh


First printed September 2000

10 9 8 7 6 5 4 3 2 1

Printed in the United States of America


Hardcover ISBN: 0-9678590-1-8
Softcover ISBN: 0-9678590-2-6

LCCN: 00-107405

# Contents

Foreword • **xi**
Preface • **xiii**
Jascha Heifetz • **xvii**

Preludio • **1**
The First Year *(1974 - 1975)* • **7**
The Second Year *(1975 - 1976)* • **31**
The Third Year *(1976 - 1977)* • **45**
Summertime *(1977 - 1978)* • **59**
Sea Murmurs: At Malibu • **63**
Finale of the Student Years *(1978-1979)* • **71**
Encore: We Meet Again • **81**
Gifts • **95**
Lifelong Friendship • **103**
Final Understanding • **109**
Coda • **111**
Wit and Wisdom of Jascha Heifetz • **113**

The Heifetz Caprices: Photo Album • **129**

# Foreword

When the American Record Guide sent me a review copy of Sherry Kloss's CD *Forgotten Gems*, a recording of two dozen short pieces that were favorites of Jascha Heifetz, I knew that I had been given something very special. Her personal way of playing these little pieces gave me the sense that she was holding a sort of musical secret passed to her in trust by Jascha Heifetz. It was clear to me that Sherry Kloss had something extraordinary and valuable in her heart, and I believe Jascha Heifetz saw that too. I felt that through Sherry Kloss I could really get to understand something about Jascha Heifetz.

I finally met Sherry in 1995 when she gave a Master Class in Chicago. She told several stories about what it was like to meet, study with, and work as the assistant to Jascha Heifetz. After the class I encouraged her to write her stories down and offered to help organize them. About a year later an envelope arrived with material she had written. I felt extremely honored and challenged to help begin the process of putting her story together.

Many critics have written about Jascha Heifetz as a reserved person, and some have presented his personality as cold and removed. I have always loved his playing and considered it odd that such a warm, complicated, sensitive, and even vulnerable artist could really be the person his critics described. On the other hand, those who really knew him speak of him with great admiration. It seems only a few people really knew him. When Sherry talked about her mentor during the class, it became clear to me that she was a person whom Heifetz admired and trusted. She was one who truly knew and understood the character of the man.

Sherry Kloss's memories of her association with Jascha Heifetz are a vital link between the "old" musical world and the present. Devoted to passing down a musical tradition, Heifetz said, "An artist is entrusted with something for a brief time. It is an artist's duty to hand it on, like those Greek runners who passed on the lighted torch one to another." Sherry Kloss passes the Heifetz torch to all of us not only by touching audiences with her own superb artistry but also by opening the door to the traditions of the Heifetz classroom so that we, too, may learn the lessons Heifetz taught.

—Elaine Fine, Reviewer,
*American Record Guide*

# Preface

The violin became my friend at age nine. My first major appearance occurred with the Pittsburgh Symphony at the age of twelve. The combination of a cantorial family on my mother's side and the dedication, discipline and fine detail which I observed in my father, a master watchmaker, laid the foundation for my musical odyssey.

By the time I entered college, there had been established within me an affinity for expression through music. Initiation into the Mu Phi Epsilon professional sorority (now a fraternity) at the School of Music at Duquesne University in Pittsburgh, Pennsylvania, offered me a special camaraderie with others whose lives were devoted to music with the creed of "Music, Friendship, and Harmony." Little did I know that my participation in the sorority would provide me with the experience of a lifetime and direct me to my life's work. That experience came in the form of the Sterling Staff International Competition, which offers its winners concert engagements throughout the United States. From Duquesne to New York's Juilliard to Boston University, from Europe to Australia, I have searched for the best of teachers and musical experiences. When I met Jascha Heifetz in August of 1974, my own musical gifts began to take on a new dimension.

As a finalist in the Sterling Staff International Competition of 1974, I would travel from Boston to Palm Springs to compete. Jascha Heifetz lived and taught violin in Southern California, and I decided to write him a note. Yet, after three unsatisfying drafts, my words seemed so inane and presumptuous that I could not mail the letter. Let fate take its course, I thought. *And so it did:* I was chosen a winner in the string category by a jury composed of Earl Wild, concert pianist; Robert Sherman, *New York Times* and Music Director of WQXR in New York; Stella Roman, former Metropolitan Opera diva; John LaMontaine, Pulitzer Prize composer and NBC Orchestra pianist; Dr. Oliver Daniel, Vice President of Broadcast Music, Inc.; and Dr. Grant Beglarian, Dean of the Southern California School of Music, who invited me to audition for Jascha Heifetz. Within two weeks I was a member of the Heifetz Master Class.

Mr. Heifetz, the artist, the teacher, and the man, presented a completely new musical world to me. A combination of strong principles, great artistry and devoted teaching, this man shared with his students a tradition which he was largely responsible for creating. He spent the latter years of his life teaching, thus he ensured that the violinist's most glorious era, from Leopold Auer and Fritz Kreisler to Jascha Heifetz, would continue to live. His carefully chosen students were expected to meet the rigorous requirements demanded by his own example. Classes usually contained from four to eight, but Mr. Heifetz was concerned with the quality of his students and with his special interest in each one, not with the number of pupils he attracted. We met twice a week from 11 a.m. to 4 p.m. in a formal classroom setting. Hard work and strong individuality were a must in presenting huge amounts of repertoire at great speed. There was sight reading and chamber music in addition to the study of viola and piano. He showed us the use of colors, contrasting styles, phrasing and spontaneous interpretation.

Each class had a magical aura, but the most special moment for me occurred when the situation called for a demonstration. He would rise from his chair with the grace of nobility and slowly walk to his violin case with a presence that drew us into his every movement. He would take out the violin, tighten the bow, and tune up the strings. I waited with great anticipation for the sounds which would illuminate an idea. Whether it was the deep intensity of late Beethoven or castanet dancers clicking their heels in DeFalla, he always communicated his point without words. His eyes would twinkle when a student captured the essence of what he had "said," and the room was charged with magnetic energy.

I had the incredible opportunity to combine this advanced study with the professional commitments presented to me as a winner of the Sterling Staff International Competition. For five years I studied in this intense situation, accumulating information and beautiful sounds to sustain me for the rest of my life. When Mr. Heifetz asked me to become his assistant, my role took on still more meaning. I screened prospective students and, if they were accepted, prepared them for class. My judgments of students and choice of their repertoire were an integral part of the success of the entire program. The Heifetz Class was a fascinating mix of nationalities, personalities and musical temperaments. This was *the* experience of a lifetime.

After the death of Jascha Heifetz in December of 1987, I learned that he had willed to me his 1736 Carlo Tononi violin and François Tourte bow. Mr. Heifetz has assured that his legacy will continue to live through me during my lifetime. Every performance I give and each lesson I teach carries with it Jascha Heifetz's special message. My fervent desire is that his message will be perpetuated forever through those whose lives he has touched. To this end I am totally committed.

I thank all of those whose belief, support and guidance nurtured my development, from the former Powers model in Indianapolis, who instructed me on stage graces, to the voice professor in Emporia, Kansas, who managed to add an additional performance on a major concert series in order to present me to her community. To all of my teachers I owe a debt of gratitude. I was fortunate enough to be exposed to many who influenced me over the years, including Mischa Mischakov, Louis Persinger, Felix Galimir, Robert Mann, Eugene Lehner and Franco Gulli. And to those teachers who patiently devoted themselves to me on a regular basis, I am forever grateful: George J. Gregus, Jack Goldman, Ferdinand Pranzatelli, Oleg Kovalenko, Raymond Montoni, Ivan Galamian, Sally Thomas, Joseph Silverstein, Tibor Varga, Nathan Milstein and Jascha Heifetz. I look forward to sharing my art and the magnificent sounds of the Heifetz-Tononi with all those who wish to revel in the joys and majesty of the musical experience.

# Jascha Heifetz

"In all my fifty years of violin teaching,
I have never known such precocity."
—Leopold Auer

Jascha Heifetz was born in Vilnius, Lithuania, at the beginning of the 20th century. His father Ruvin, concertmaster of the Vilna Symphonic Orchestra, was his first violin teacher. After two years of study with his father, the five-year-old Jascha began lessons at the Vilnius Imperial School of Music with Iliya Malkin, an old friend of his father, who had been a student of the great Hungarian teacher, Leopold Auer. At the age of six, Jascha began performing publicly. In 1910, when he entered Auer's class at the St. Petersburg Conservatory, he was already an experienced violinist. Although his formal musical education ended when he was still a teenager, he was already astonishing audiences all over Europe. Because of the political turmoil created by the Bolsheviks, he and his family fled their homeland and arrived in the United States. The young Heifetz made his sensational New York Carnegie Hall debut Saturday afternoon, October 27, 1917, at the age of sixteen, establishing his playing as the new standard in violin mastery. Famed violinists of the day nervously spoke of burning their instruments upon hearing him play.

Heifetz became a United States citizen in 1925 as he launched a career of world tours that drew capacity crowds. He continued to mesmerize audiences while becoming a popular icon, appearing in films, on radio, and on TV with many of the popular performers of the day, including Jack Benny and Bing Crosby.

Veterans recall his many performances for the troops during World War II, even one performance in a concert hall in Krefeld, Germany, where one wall of the hall had been blown out.

Demonstrating great pride in being an American, he was an active force in social issues, including the rights of artists (the formation of the American Guild of Musical Artists [AGMA]), and the creation of the emergency telephone number 911. He commissioned, championed, performed and recorded works of composers that elevated the music to stellar heights. His towering violinistic genius and personal style placed an indelible stamp upon everything he played.

He did not begin to teach until he felt he was ready to devote time away from his performance career. In 1958 he taught at the University of California, Los Angeles, for a year, and in 1961 he became Professor of Violin at the University of Southern California, where he remained until 1985. His last public performance in 1972 was a benefit concert for the School of Music, University of Southern California, at the Dorothy Chandler Pavilion, where he played to a standing-room-only audience. He continued to devote himself totally to his pupils until he retired from teaching in 1986. Besides his performing and teaching, he is known for over 100 transcriptions for violin and piano.

He died in Los Angeles on December 10, 1987, shortly after my last visit with him. His recordings are classics. His contribution to musical history is now a legend.

**LAUGH PARADE**

by Bill Hoest

"$120.34 for a tune-up? Who tuned it, Jascha Heifetz?"

# Jascha Heifetz
## Through My Eyes

School of Music
University of Southern California

# The class of
# JASCHA HEIFETZ for accomplished violinists

Violinists from the United States and abroad who are prepared to meet the demands and standards of the Heifetz class are invited to submit applications for consideration by Mr. Heifetz. Scholarships are available.

Mr. Heifetz will personally audition chosen finalists after a preliminary screening. The decision for admission to the class rests solely with Mr. Heifetz.

Applicants will be notified to appear for audition in Los Angeles.

Suggested repertoire

1. One Sonata or Partita for Unaccompanied Violin by J.S. Bach.
2. Brahms D Minor Sonata for Violin and Piano.
3. One concerto, chosen from the following composers: Mozart, Mendelssohn, Beethoven, Brahms, Sibelius, Prokofiev, Tchaikovsky, etc.
4. One work of candidate's choice.
5. Paganini Caprice No. 17.
6. Scales – all forms.

A pianist will be provided.

# Preludio

"You have to know the rules
before you can break them."
—Referring to performance of Bach
Unaccompanied Sonatas and Partitas

"How would you like to meet Jascha Heifetz?" The question was posed to me by Grant Beglarian, Dean of the University of Southern California School of Performing Arts, in August of 1974, just after I had won a competition in Palm Springs.

With great excitement I answered "yes," but immediately began to wonder how I could be *ready* to present myself to this legendary master of the violin. I couldn't have imagined then how the proposition of "being ready" would become such a part of my future association with the man, nor how it would become a haunting philosophical question for me in my lifetime. What does "being ready" really mean?

I had heard much about the intense standards to be met for admission into the elite Master Class of Jascha Heifetz, so I spent the next days working on scales. Scales were rumored the downfall of most audition candidates, but although my previous teachers believed in them, I feared that nothing could have prepared me to play them for Mr. Heifetz. I instinctively understood that what I would present would be Sherry Kloss. No amount of work could change what I was.

When I arrived at Mr. Heifetz's beach home in Malibu for the audition on Saturday, August 31, 1974, the master greeted me wearing colorful Jamaican shorts, a polo shirt, sandals, sunglasses and a floppy hat. So this was California beach wear, I thought, a wild contrast to the Bostonian style of dress to which I was accustomed. This was my introduction to Jascha Heifetz the person, not just a face on a record jacket. He invited me to join him outdoors in the pleasant ocean air, and then, despite the casual ambiance, conducted a brief but probing interview which covered not only my musical but also my personal background. He asked about my upbringing, and I told him about my immigrant parents, Ben, a watchmaker, and Myrna, a piano teacher, both Polish Jews, and about my younger brother Herb, a jazz flutist in pre-medical training, his aspirations, and my relationship with him. This was his way of sizing me up, finding out about my family, and learning about my close relationship with my brother. Such information reflected the thoroughness of his interview, which was as precise in its own way as his attention to every detail of his appearance.

The moment I saw the man I was astonished to discover a resemblance to my father, and as he proceeded with the interview, I became aware of other uncanny similarities to my dad: his insistence upon precision, his demeanor, and his knowing silence. At this first meeting, my comparison of the two men was only a momentary thought, for I was nervously involved in my audition. As the years passed, however, my every interaction with the man would strengthen the comparison. How much they were alike!

After learning of my Polish heritage, he asked if I spoke the language. When I responded enthusiastically with my limited vocabulary, *"Jak sie masz,"* he continued to speak Polish, but I had to confess that I had reached the end of my contribution in that language. My Polish vocabulary was no match for my good intentions. I was anxious to get on with the audition, and I knew that he noticed.

"Is there anything I can do for you?" he asked. "Would you

like some refreshment?" The thought of ingesting anything, even water, was out of the question in my state of excitement.

"No, thank you," I replied.

I felt my eyes growing huge and my voice growing small and halting. "I'd like to get this over with," I said, trying desperately not to sound desperate. After opening the screen door, he directed me inside and gestured for me to place my violin on a daybed located in the far right corner of the room, while he sat next to a small table near the window facing the beach. Hanging on the wall above the daybed was a collection of interesting looking, colorful international hats which caught my attention. I barely remember unpacking my violin and tightening the bow. After that, everything became a blur and seemed unreal. When the pianist, Ayke Agus, had taken her place at the little upright piano on the other side of the room, he asked what I had brought to play. Then he suggested "whatever you play the best." That was a difficult decision, considering for whom I was about to perform!

I had presented two pages of the Glazunov *Concerto* when he asked me to "please remove your watch . . . it's a distraction, you know," and then I continued with one half page of the *Adagio* from the Bach *Unaccompanied Sonata in G Minor*. I suddenly became aware of a tapping sound coming from Mr. Heifetz's direction indicating that he wished me to stop. He began to sing rhythmic passages and asked me to duplicate on the violin the passage in question. We went through this exercise at least four times before I said, "Obviously I'm doing something wrong, and I don't know what it is."

"You are right," he said. "Wrong rhythm." We worked on that until it was corrected.

Then in the key of C Major he sang the theme of the Beethoven *Sonata in C Minor* and asked me, "What's wrong with that?"

In my state of anxiety I thought I must be hearing incorrectly;

however, despite my feeling that I was in the midst of a "trial," my musical ear did not fail me. I identified the discrepancy between the minor 3rd which Beethoven had written and the glaring major 3rd Mr. Heifetz was singing for me, but it was a little daunting for me to accuse the great Jascha Heifetz of singing out of tune. Aha! He was testing my ear! Then a most unusual thing occurred. There was a knock at the door. The momentum of the audition was instantly diminished as we all searched out the sound with our eyes. Standing outside was a plumber in full regalia, tools in hand.

"Ah, I do think the plumber has arrived," Mr. Heifetz said, asking to be excused. He led the handyman through the hallway and up the stairs. I, meanwhile, was greatly relieved to rid myself of some chewing gum in my mouth, which I had become embarrassingly aware of as I was playing. And besides, I could gather my inner forces for the most dreaded part of the Heifetz audition: *the scales.*

When he returned, he asked me to play the F-sharp Major scale. I began in the high position on the G string and completed it successfully.

"Now a G-flat Major," he said with a stoical look as he motioned me to continue the same pace.

I played the same fingerings as I had for the F-sharp scale.

"No, no, no! The G-flat scale has an G-flat fingering. Start in the first position with the third finger," he suggested.

And so I did. Of course, I knew how to begin this one, but goodness only knew how I would reach the heights in tempo. He continued to tap the pulse while I fumbled my way up with some pretty "interesting" fingerings. When I arrived home to the G-flat first position, he said, "You need work on your scales."

After I finished, he asked, "Why do you want to be in my class?"

A little astonished by the directness of the question at the time, I was to understand in retrospect that my answer may have been the most important part of the audition. "I was hoping I could learn something," I heard myself blurting out.

He rose from his chair, walked over to me, and said, "I can't promise you that. You are old, you know, but I would like to have you in my class very much." I was 28 years old. Viewing myself as "old" had not yet ever been a consideration for me! Then he patted me on the shoulder and asked, "Do you play Ping-Pong?"

Thus began an association with the great Jascha Heifetz that continued until his death in December of 1987.

# The First Year
(1974 - 1975)

"Keep your eyes on what you are doing,
or you may have an accident."
—In advising players who had roaming
or closed eyes as they played

The Jascha Heifetz Master Class met on the second floor of the Virginia Ramo Music Building of the University of Southern California every Tuesday and Friday from 11:00 a.m. to 4:00 p.m. throughout the academic year. The building had been built with Mr. Heifetz especially in mind by Simon and Virginia Ramo, well-known Los Angeles philanthropists. When I arrived for my first class on October 8, 1974, I learned from some of the "veteran" students who were waiting with me that a rear window on the second floor provided a perfect view of the parking lot into which Mr. Heifetz would drive his beautiful black and silver Bentley (originally owned by Gary Cooper). His specially marked parking space was located at the outer edge of the lot. We all watched his arrival ritual. To a new student like me it was a thrilling experience just to see the regal manner in which Mr. Heifetz carried himself. He wore an overcoat and hat, carried a walking stick (which, I later learned, had been given to him by his teacher, Leopold Auer). One of the male students waiting for him in the parking lot greeted him with an offer to help with whatever he was carrying.

After disappearing into the building, he walked up the outer stairs (he did not use the elevator) and unlocked the classroom door, which opened into a small entry hallway. To the right was a restroom, and to the left was Mr. Heifetz's greenroom. It contained a desk, chairs, a sofa, a heart-shaped maple telephone table, and another table shaped like an artist's palette. One piece of furniture in the room that would come to have great meaning for me was a beautiful little blond upright Knight piano.

After Mr. Heifetz entered the inner hallway, the door closed behind him and we students waited what seemed to be a very long time before his assistant, Claire Hodgkins, asked us to come in. (Several years later, when I became his assistant, I learned that during this time Mr. Heifetz readied himself for class. His preparation included some light warm-ups such as slow bows and slow scales.) Before entering the classroom, the women checked their make-up, hairdos and general appearance while the men combed their hair and straightened their ties. It was obvious that grooming was important, and I worried about whether the clothes I had chosen passed the guidelines of "class protocol."

At the end of the entry hallway was the commodious classroom containing a grand piano to the left and Mr. Heifetz's large desk to the right. On the desk lay a somewhat battered car antenna (often kept tucked away in a desk drawer), which students came to recognize as one of his teaching tools. Behind the desk was a large chair, and to either side of the desk were two very comfortable looking, large chairs. (I could only surmise that they were comfortable, for they were "guest" chairs, and I never sat in them.) From his desk chair he could look through a window at a pine tree especially planted by Mrs. Virginia Ramo so that he could see it from where he worked. For students and auditors the room contained orange, padded folding armchairs. Otherwise, the decor consisted of some carefully chosen dieffenbachia plants and memorabilia, including on one wall a framed program of a celebration for Fritz Kreisler at

The Bohemians, a professional musicians' club in New York, along with Kreisler's photo. I was impressed by Mr. Heifetz's meticulous attention to the decor of his classroom, and I still enjoy a cutting from one of those plants.

As each of us entered the room, Mr. Heifetz greeted us with his piercing, seemingly all-knowing eyes and said, "Good morning." I was to learn that his scrutiny and greeting were both part of his sincere concern for the well-being of each of his students. His power as a mentor went far beyond his influence on our musical skills. There is no question that one of the reasons I was able to respond to and survive the rigorous demands of my teacher was that I related to his demands in the same way that I had related to the demands of my own upbringing. I felt comfortable with his challenges. I had traveled the world in pursuit of learning and inspiration, and I had been fortunate to have wonderful teachers. Each one of them had prepared me in some special way to meet this new challenge. The world of Heifetz was a whole different environment. Now, at long last, I felt as if I had come home.

I later came to understand that Mr. Heifetz usually knew the emotional state of each one of his students at any given moment. It was no use to avoid eye contact when he greeted us or to try to conceal our feelings or problems from him. The result of his careful scrutiny was that he knew what to expect from each of us. He told me five years later, after I had become his assistant, "Sherry, I know my customers." He need not have told me that, for by that time I had learned from experience that he did, indeed, know us.

On that first day we placed our violins on a large table behind the piano and waited for Mr. Heifetz's introductory words. During the first class of each new year he gave a warm welcome to new students and radiated an unmistakable twinkle of the eye to those who were "veterans."

He might ask someone, "So, how was your summer?" After some responses, he would ask, "Anyone else have anything to contribute?"

After looking around at all the students, he noted a new haircut. "Well . . . um . . . it's not . . . unbecoming."

Then, when he was ready to begin, he asked, "Who's ready?"

It was all part of his plan. Mr. Heifetz did little, I was to learn, that was not carefully calculated to produce results from his students. "Ready," to Mr. Heifetz, meant the ability to exhibit a level of understanding of the music, its style, its lilt and its message. He did not necessarily expect perfect playing nor was he impressed by excessive display of temperament. In his teaching he devoted himself tirelessly and, yes, sometimes abruptly, to accomplishing these qualities. He knew after just a few notes whether or not a piece was "ready."

I was stunned by the question, "Who's ready?" In my heart I never felt ready. I became involved in an intellectual struggle to understand what "being ready" meant. When is one ready? How is one ready? What is ready? Can anything ever be "ready" to present to Jascha Heifetz? Defining the word was to become, for me, a pervasive philosophical question like, "What's life all about?" or "Why do we exist?" The question "When am I ready?" would haunt me for many years.

I was totally absorbed by Mr. Heifetz and the class. I learned quickly that the dynamics of the class were an important part of its flow. The dynamics were crucial in determining whether a class would be tense or less tense. Although each lesson was carefully planned, Mr. Heifetz's response to students was always spontaneous, which courted a reciprocal spontaneity in each one of us.

I recall once after the morning greeting, Mr. Heifetz, a fair and honest man, turned his head forcefully to face a particular student. Sternly, he said, "I have never been a fan of hallway gossip . . . and don't intend to include those who partake of this sort of thing in my class." Only the male student with the purple face understood what had caused Mr. Heifetz to deliver the message. Needless to say, the tenor of the class remained strained for the first part of that day.

Another incident involved one of the finest students in the class, a young man from Korea who was always respectful and smiling. The young man had been carrying a bulky briefcase to class for some time, and one day Mr. Heifetz, in the middle of class, suddenly side-stepped his way from the piano to the student's desk and stood in front of the young man. "May I?" he asked, pointing to the bulging briefcase.

A huge cheerful smile graced the student's face.

"Rather heavy, I would say," Mr. Heifetz commented as he lifted the bag in an exact imitation of the student. "What do you carry in here? Bibles?"

I could hardly control my laughter. How did he know that the student had become a Jehovah's Witness who spent ample time (too ample, evidently, to suit Mr. Heifetz) "spreading the word" from door to door? How could he know such a thing? This classroom revelation, unlike some of the harsher reprimands, left us all with a smile and firmly established the feeling that I had always sensed—that Mr. Heifetz became our conscience as well as our teacher.

Every moment of these classes was mentally and emotionally charged. Mr. Heifetz's teaching techniques and idiosyncrasies often amused me and sometimes surprised me, but always fascinated me. Although I was nervous for every class, I loved each moment. His musical greatness and personal sincerity inspired us, and when one of his creative suggestions did not produce the result he hoped for, he would quietly get up from his desk and, without speaking, walk regally to the piano where his violin rested. He would play only to demonstrate a point of style, never to command us as an audience. He was capable of jumping into the middle of a passage, totally aware of what a particular student needed to be shown. He was the master of his instrument, the music, the moment and the needs of his students. Sometimes he left me breathless during these interventions where musical sounds rather than words were the means of communication. What Mr. Heifetz wanted most was to help us cultivate our own musical individuality.

I learned quickly during those first weeks of study that students were responsible for major and minor scales in all combinations—thirds, sixths, octaves, fingered octaves and tenths—beginning from any given degree of a scale. All arpeggios (notes of a broken chord played in rapid succession) were to be concluded in staccato bowing. In addition to the music that we prepared for class, at any time we might be asked to play all of the Bach unaccompanied sonatas and partitas and at least twelve Paganini caprices from memory. In addition, all students had to study piano, and though we had Ayke Agus as our resident pianist, we would be asked occasionally to provide accompaniment, without preparation, for another student. Chamber music was a regular class activity, and although cellists were invited to participate with the class on these occasions, violists were not invited because we violinists were expected to step into that role with ease. During the early years of the class, the renowned violist William Primrose provided instruction on the instrument. At semester's end there were viola and piano exams which our teacher attended.

Gradually I became accustomed to Mr. Heifetz's "little twists" of the day. They were all part of his teaching style—providing variety and surprise to keep us on our toes. He sometimes called upon a student to play without advance preparation (an instant of adrenaline rush) or to read Mozart or Schubert piano duos for four hands (sometimes Mr. Heifetz was the other pianist). On these occasions he discovered areas about

## JASCHA HEIFETZ CLASS REPETOIRE (CONCERTI)

| | |
|---|---|
| ELGAR | SPOHR (#8 GESANGSCENE) |
| WALTON | BEETHOVEN |
| SIBELIUS | TSCHAIKOWSKY |
| GLAZOUNOFF | BRAHMS |
| MENDELSSOHN | PROKOFIEV (G&D) |
| BRUCH (G & D | WIENIAWSKI (D MINOR) |
|   & SCOTTISH FANTASY) | HINDEMITH (1939) |
| GOLDMARK | ROZSA |
| MOZART (A.D.E.) | PAGANINI |
| BACH (DOUBLE, A & E) | ERNST |
| SAINT-SAENS (B) | NARDINI (E MINOR) |
| LALO (SPANISH SYMPHONY) | GRUENBERG |
| CONUS | KORNGOLD |
| VIEUXTEMPS (#4 & 5) | LIAPOUNOFF |
| CASTELNUOVO TEDESCO (#2) | |

a student's ability or lack of it that might need to be addressed. A surprise twist might involve sight reading one of two voices of the *Rhythmic Etudes* of Martinu with the piano playing the other voice. As if these exercises weren't tough enough to decode in comfortable circumstances, we had to stand behind the pianist and read from the score of the piano rack a fair distance away. He might request a student to play a movement of unaccompanied Bach or to read a concerto. Sometimes, when a composer had sent a work to Mr. Heifetz for consideration and critique, we would be the ones to read through the work. The unexpected events of each class meeting were an important part of the exhilaration of the Heifetz experience.

Sight reading was a regular exercise in the class. Mr. Heifetz would ask his assistant to choose appropriate works from our class library to be "read" by students. These works might be anything from Spohr or Wieniawski duets to the Conus Concerto. We were expected to play these pieces straight through to the end while Mr. Heifetz tapped his car antenna on the top of his desk as a constant reminder of the ongoing pulse. Over time this tapping had beaten deep scars into the desk, which at a later date had to be refinished.

## JASCHA HEIFETZ CLASS REPETOIRE (SONATAS)

HANDEL (E.D.&A. (BREITKOPH & HAERTEL)
BEETHOVEN (ALL)
SCHUMANN (#1) A-MINOR (AUGENER, LTD.)
MOZART (#8, 10 & 15)           CESAR FRANCK
GRIEG (C-MINOR & G MAJOR)      TARTINI (G MINOR)
STRAUSS                        LOCATELLI (F MINOR)
BLOCH (1ST, 2ND) POEME MYSTIQUE
ENESCO (#2)                    DEBUSSY
MEDTNER (#1)                   SAINT-SAENS (#1)
TREMAIS (F MINOR)              BRAHMS
FERGUSON                       HINDEMITH
FAURE                          PIERNE
RESPIGHI (B MINOR)             LECLAIR
PIZETTI

### (SMALL PIECES)

| | |
|---|---|
| CAPRICE #24 | PAGANINI - AUER |
| CAPRICE #13 | PAGANINI - KREISLER |
| CAPRICE #20 | PAGANINI - KREISLER |
| UN POCO TRISTE | JOSEPH SUK |
| BURLESCA | JOSEPH SUK |
| SLAVONIC DANCES (G & E) | DVORAK - KREISLER |
| CAPRICEUSE | ELGAR |
| THE BUMBLE BEE | R. KORSAKOFF - HEIFETZ |
| PERPETUAL MOTION | NOVACEK - RIES, PAGANINI, CECIL BURLEIGH |
| WAVES AT PLAY | GRASSE |
| MALAGUENA & HABANERA | SARASATE |
| ZAPATEADO | SARASATE |
| INTRO. & TARANTELLE | SARASATE |
| HEBREW MELODY | ACHRON |
| HEBREW DANCE | ACHRON |

| | |
|---|---|
| AVE MARIA | SCHUBERT |
| HORA STACCATO | DINICU - J.H. |
| NOCTURNE (D) | CHOPIN |
| ALT - WIEN | GODOWSKY - J.H. |
| RECITATIVE & SCHERZO | KREISLER (CHARLES FOLEY) |
| BAAL SHEM (NIGUN) | BLOCH |
| HUNGARIAN DANCES (1,7,11) ETC. | BRAHMS |
| SCHERZO TARANTELLE | WIENIAWSKI |
| RONDO | SCHUBERT (FRIEDBERG) |
| RONDO | MOZART (KREISLER) |
| 2 POLONAISES | WIENIAWSKI |
| AIR | BACH |
| NOCTURNE | SZYMANOWSKI |
| CHANT DE ROXANE | SZYMANOWSKI |
| A LA VALSE | VICTOR HERBERT |
| BANJO & FIDDLE | KROLL |
| MELODIE | TSCHAIKOWSKY |
| PRELUDES & PORGY & BESS | GERSHWIN - J.H. |
| SUMARE | MILHAUD |
| CORCOVADO | MILHAUD |
| PRELUDES ( 1 & 2) | SHOSTAKOVITCH |
| MELODIE | GLUCK-HEIFETZ |
| CHORUS OF DERVISHES | BEETHOVEN - AUER |
| LA CHASSE | CARTIER (KREISLER) |
| ON WINGS OF SONG | MENDELSSOHN |
| CAPRICCIO - VALSE | WIENIAWSKI |
| NOCTURNE | SIBELIUS |
| MINUETTO | MOZART |
| VIENNESE | GODOWSKY |
| ESTRELLITA | PONCE - J.H. |
| GUITARRE | MOSZKOWSKI |
| RONDE DES LUTINS | BAZZINI |
| EN BATEAU | DEBUSSY |
| IL PLEURE DANS MON COEUR | DEBUSSY |
| LA FILLE AU CHEVEAU, (GIRL WITH THE FLAXEN HAIR) | DEBUSSY |
| PIECE EN FORME DE HABANERA | RAVEL |

## (MISCELLANEOUS)

| | |
|---|---|
| INTR & RONDO CAPRICCIOSO | SAINT - SAENS |
| HAVANAISE | SAINT - SAENS |
| GYPSY AIRS | SARASATE |
| TZIGANE | RAVEL |
| CHACONNE | VITALI (ARR. BY |
| (ALSO WITH ORGAN - RESPIGHI) | LEOPOLD CHARLIER- |
| | BREITKOPH & HAERTEL |
| LARK | CASTELNUOVO-TEDESCO |
| | (EDITED BY J.H.) |
| FIGARO | CASTELNUOVO-TEDESCO |
| | (EDITED BY HEIFETZ) |
| RURALIA HUNGARICA | DOHNANYI (CARL |
| (3 COMPOSITIONS) | FISCHER, INC.) |
| HEXAPODA | ROBERT RUSSELL |
| | BENNETT |
| LA FOLIA | CORELLI |
| SONATINAS | SCHUBERT |
| DEVIL'S TRILL | TARTINI |
| SUITE | VIVALDI (BUSCH) |
| POEME | CHAUSSON |
| BALLAD & POLONAISE | VIEUXTEMPS |
| TALLAHASSE SUITE | SCOTT |
| MUCH ADO ABOUT NOTHING | KORNGOLD |
| SONATENSATZ | BRAHMS |
| VALSE | TCHAIKOWSKY |
| SERENADE MELANCHOLIQUE | TCHAIKOWSKY |
| TWO ROMANCES | BEETHOVEN |
| WITCHES DANCE | PAGANINI |
| CARMEN FANTASY | BIZET - WAXMAN |
| FANTASY | SCHUBERT |

All of these demanding exercises required us to be prepared for surprises. He was building our self-confidence and preparing us to accept daunting challenges without flinching. I remember one time when a Polish student, Piotr (Peter) Janowsky, played a violin work, followed by the viola part of

Loeffler's *Trio for Oboe, Viola, and Piano,* and then concluded by dashing off a piece at the piano. He was brilliant! When he finished, Mr. Heifetz asked his assistant to choose something unfamiliar from our music library for the student to play at sight on the violin. Mr. Heifetz asked if he knew the chosen piece, and when he silently indicated "no," Mr. Heifetz asked him to play it with the pianist accompanying him. The suspense increased again at the end of his reading when Mr. Heifetz removed the music from the stand and asked that the work now be played from memory. Amazingly, he did it. This was the kind of student that truly interested our teacher.

---

**TEACHING AID OF MR. HEIFETZ, OFTEN READ TO THE CLASS**

Donington also quoted Johann Mattheson's famous list. Mattheson was a major composer and a friend of Handel, and he wrote, in 1713, that everything could be portrayed in music: "love, jealousy, hatred, gentleness, impatience, lust, indifference, fear, vengeance, fortitude, timidity, magnanimity, horror, dignity, baseness, splendor, indigence, pride, humility, joy, laughter, weeping, mirth, pain, happiness, despair, storm, tranquility, even heaven and earth, sea and hell—together with all the actions in which men participate." Students should be made to memorize this passage. It could be a corrective against the dry, metrically exact, objective manner in which so much Bach is played.

---

Another aspect of Mr. Heifetz's teaching was his love of the "itsy-bitsy" (the three or four-minute "character" piece, so popular a hundred years ago). He offered this "prize" only after he felt a student had all the musical staples in order (scales, *etudes,* Bach, Beethoven, *concerti*). Only then would he put one of these "itsy-bitsies" on the music stand and say, "This is a good one for you." The student played the piece on the spot and inevitably went home with a treat . . . a new reward.

The most special part of the Heifetz phenomenon was observing his ability to convey his magical, stylistic understanding of music to the students. He could transport us to a place where we suddenly experienced things that we might never have known or considered because of our preoccupation with some more immediate violinistic technical matter. He had an unforgettable way with the short piece. For me, these short pieces were little gems. I began compiling a list of these works, and years later released my first recording entitled *Forgotten Gems,* a collection of these jewels. I recall one class when I had presented Jeno Hubay's *Zephyr.* Mr. Heifetz's eyes glinted with excitement as Ayke began the tricky piano opening of this devilish number. As he worked with me, I suddenly heard the "wssiss" of the wind. Then, as we worked on other short pieces, he caused me to feel the pathos of the cantorial *Nigun* or demonstrated with a click of his heels and a snap of his fingers how DeFalla's *Danse Espagnole* communicates passion with insistent rhythm. He created for me the solace of Ponce's *Estrellita* and the sarcastic wit of Prokofiev's *Masks.* Percy Grainger's *Molly on the Shore* transformed a city classroom into a corner square with country folks dancing the Irish reel. He even led me to understand the sad humor of a donkey's lot in life in Ibert's *The Little Donkey.* He had a scenario for every "little gem" and made us see and feel the world that the music conveyed. We learned that within these little works a world of information was waiting to be interpreted. The artist does not have twenty minutes to convey the message. A mere few minutes must tell it all.

As a contrast to these intense and arduous moments of enlightenment, he also showed a devilish sense of humor. With a mixture of pupils from all over the world, he derived well-intentioned pleasure from imitating the many accents and pronunciations of his students. He loved to mimic my Pittsburgh accent, always with a twinkling smile on his face. On more than one occasion, when the task that he had set for me caused me to surrender to the expression "I can't" (pronounced "kehnt" in Pittsburghese), Mr. Heifetz would say, "*Kehnt! Kehnt! Kehnt!* Someone in this class *sez* she *kehnt* play a staccato bowing and then proceeds to play a perfect one. But she *kehnt* do it!" Even as he ridiculed my accent, he provided me with a compliment that armed me with confidence for the next class. It was all part of the Heifetz magic.

And there were other times when Mr. Heifetz had to use his magic to deal with my recurrent lapses of confidence. Long before I met Mr. Heifetz, I had been told by a teacher that some people can play Bach and some can't (or *kehnt*). Affected by that observation, I did not feel very comfortable playing Bach. Then one day in class Mr. Heifetz asked me to "play some Bach." Tenuously I played the first movement and part of the fugue from the unaccompanied *Sonata in A Minor*. He responded by saying, "Hmm, we will be spending some time on this one."

I heard myself saying aloud, "Oh, no, not again. I am sick of this Bach." Then I was instantly embarrassed to have revealed my trepidation. I steeled myself for his reply.

With a determination too enormous for me to resist, he said simply, "You will stay on this one and the others until you play Bach well. No short pieces until then." He knew that my particular love of the short piece would provide the incentive I needed to master the depths of Bach. The subtleties of 32nd and 16th note rhythms, the contrast in the phrasing articulations of dots and slurs, and the counterpoint of the inner voices were awaiting my further discovery. There was to be no saying "I *kehnt.*"

Then, after his firm admonition, delivered with a degree of severity, he put me at ease by telling a story of how he had in concert begun playing the Bach *A Minor Fugue* and inadvertently jumped into the shorter G Minor. "The G Minor! It was the shortest unaccompanied violin fugue in history and I once made it the longest," he recalled. His sense of humor, one of his most powerful teaching tools, made me smile and relieved the tension of the moment. His teaching genius prevailed once again, and I left determined to master the Bach.

Several classes later Mr. Heifetz asked me, "How is Bach coming along? Do you think you can be friends?"

"I love Bach," I answered. "It is just that I can't play it."

"How are you otherwise?" he asked, totally ignoring my plaintive "can't" (or *kehnt*).

I knew what he meant. I was not to be given a reprieve, and all importunings, however subtle, were to be ignored. It was not until many classes later, after I had worked for many hours on the Bach, that he pronounced me ready to move onto other works.

After I had presented the Bach *C Major Sonata* for a class, he said, "Congratulations!"

"For what?"

"Well, you have finally gotten into it. Now you are on the road."

He always followed through when he had set a task for a student. The determination in his voice when he had ordered me to concentrate on Bach had remained like a stone wall. Only after all my devoted work could he resolve my anxiety with a compliment. It was, of course, all the reward I ever needed from him.

On another occasion during that first year Mr. Heifetz assigned me a Kreutzer *etude* with some tricky bowings. After I played it, he walked to the music stand and closed the music.

"Play it by memory," he said.

"I can't," I replied, but he ignored me and motioned for me to begin again from the top.

After attempting two lines of the *etude*, I heard him tap on his desk with the car antenna, indicating that I should stop.

"Ah," he said, "you've proven your point."

Somewhat chagrined, I could not suppress a laugh at his wit and honesty. I can still visualize that moment, and I know he enjoyed making me laugh. He was, after all, an entertainer.

Mr. Heifetz's humorously mocking sarcasm or amusing facetiousness would make me laugh, but there were times when he could be harsh to students. I remember once when a European student finished a piece in class only to be greeted with the scathing response, "Did you study with Ševčík or do you practice in a closet? Hmm . . . perhaps this will help." He suddenly produced a miniature-sized bow from behind the desk, which he handed to the student. It was hysterically funny to watch and listen to the Tchaikovsky *Concerto* played with a bowing span of some eighteen inches per stroke. After several minutes of laughter from all, Mr. Heifetz quietly suggested, "Now perhaps you would prefer to play with your own bow. Use it, won't you?" The strong suggestion ended the young man's lesson. Again, his criticism was honestly accurate, yet funny.

On another occasion a student offered a "surprise" for the class. In the middle of the piece, Mr. Heifetz stopped him and asked what he was playing. "A Kreisler minuet, an unknown work," responded the student. Mr. Heifetz answered tartly, "Maybe there is a reason why it is unknown." After this comment we were all silent. We never heard the rest of the piece.

One of Mr. Heifetz's more businesslike ways of "punishing" a student was to levy a fine. For instance, if there was a point of comprehension or definition to be clarified with more precision, Mr. Heifetz would call upon a class member whom he would playfully call "the learned one" or "the music criminologist" (someone working on a master's degree or doctorate), usually a member of the class who was adept at identifying a problem and explaining it. If the "criminologist" found a student guilty of some "infraction," and if Mr. Heifetz considered the "infraction" worthy of attention, a fine would be levied to be paid to the class treasury. (A class treasurer and class secretary had been chosen especially for these occasions.) The treasury for these occasions was a clown bank. The guilty student then placed the coin on the hand of the mechanical clown bank, and we all watched as the hand fed the mouth of the clown. It was another moment of relief from the high-powered sessions and from the otherwise demanding presence of our teacher.

A particular incident involving fines occurred one day following a recital by the great violinist Nathan Milstein. Mr. Heifetz asked who had attended the concert at the Dorothy Chandler Pavilion. Those who had not raised their hands were asked, "Why not?" and were fined five dollars each. Other fines were levied and paid to the class treasury for such things as music in poor condition, including music overly marked up with fingerings and bowings, or shabby looking music. Fines were also collected for some gap in music theory that was so obvious that any student should have known it. Mr. Heifetz would present the situation, turn to the "criminologist" for further edification, and, when convinced that a fine was deserved, he would ask the class to determine the amount. Money in the treasury was carefully accounted for and used to purchase music when needed for our Heifetz Music Library, which had become a valuable resource of the classroom.

As these first months progressed, I was becoming accustomed to the game plan that could propel the class to great heights. I loved the state of not knowing what might occur next. Though I continued to be haunted by whatever "being ready" really meant, I had become accustomed to his strict reprimands and penalties. They didn't really disturb me. In fact, I was often amused by them, but use of the term "ready" continued to haunt me from the very first time I had heard him ask the class who was "ready."

When we were asked, "Who's ready?" several hands were usually raised in response, but I never could volunteer. I had always preferred to be a listener and learner, even in my public school days back in Pittsburgh. But I soon learned that Mr. Heifetz was having none of that. He enjoyed calling on the students who did not raise their hands. While this is probably a technique common to many fine teachers, it took me a long while to figure out that he knew he could always count on the "eager beavers." They were predictable, but it was those who didn't volunteer who intrigued him! To be reticent in his class was to ensure being called upon.

Now, years later, as a teacher myself, I fully understand his desire to discover more about a shy student, but at the time, "being ready" was a concept that plagued me. I never felt "ready." Imagine having to prepare to meet the artistic demands of the great Heifetz twice a week! One can easily understand the dilemma. I not only could not feel that I was ready, but I remained mystified by those who felt that they were.

⁂

I remember, especially, the time during that first year when "being ready" was put to the test for me. I had had to miss two classes due to a concert tour through the Pacific Northwest. Following the tour I came to class completely exhausted. My "good morning" greeting to Mr. Heifetz could not camouflage the dark circles under my eyes, and I knew that, as always, he was aware of my condition. He "knew his customers." He asked me how it all went. When I told him that the concerts were fine, but that the headlines of one of the chamber music reviews blared, "Lack of Musicianship Alarming," he said, "Hm . . . can't something be done about that? On second thought, it's probably better not to know the critic . . . just probably a frustrated singer or musicologist." For certain that made me laugh as I recalled being met at the Northern California airport by the presenters of some of the performances with the following greetings: "We are in luck. Our two music critics will be in town for your concerts. One is the former editor of *Field and Stream* magazine and the other is a musicologist."

Near the end of the class he asked me to play. I had nothing new to present to him, but his sincere interest in my work demanded that I play something. So after a few moments of consideration, I stood up, unpacked my instrument, and played the Chopin-Sarasate *B-flat Nocturne,* which I had read through as a possible piece for class before leaving on tour.

After the last note, he said, "Not bad," and began to get up from behind his desk. This usually meant that he was planning to make some suggestions for fingering or phrasing, or that he would demonstrate a few notes.

Still in the midst of my philosophical struggle, I blurted out, "It's just that I don't know when something is ready."

Mr. Heifetz looked at me with his large, probing eyes and responded in a tone of voice that let the whole class know he was perturbed. "Well, Sherry, if you don't know, then perhaps you had better take up another profession. Class dismissed."

I walked weakly to my violin case to pack up my instrument, music and belongings. Still involved with the melodies of Chopin that were filling my head, I felt as if the wind had been knocked out of me by the blow that those words had struck. I was doing what I loved to do, making musical notes come to life, and yet my teacher's assessment of my personal doubts gave me *everything* to think about. Was he just being kind to me in his own way by calling attention to my own misgivings? Or had I failed to recognize a real concern emanating from my teacher during these last few minutes? His comment had startled and befuddled me. I quickly packed up my violin and music. Then I grabbed my raincoat, hoping for a quick exit.

Sneaking past the large desk where Mr. Heifetz had returned to sit down, I tried to exit the room hidden among the others as they bid their good-byes for the weekend.

"Sherry," I heard him say. I cannot explain the shame that gripped me.

He waited mercifully until the classroom had emptied and then said, "I don't like what I saw today. If you don't have confidence in yourself, how do you expect others to have confidence in you? I want to see improvement in this area. Good-bye, Sherry."

His eyes never left my own, which were filled with tears.

"Good-bye, Mr. Heifetz."

After I left the classroom, Peter Janowsky, the Polish student who had distinguished himself so brilliantly with his playing and with his ability to memorize so quickly, was waiting for me. "Sweetie, what is wrong? You played like an angel . . . so old world!"

My tears flowed freely in the presence of this sympathetic colleague.

"Won't you come to the party this evening? You probably could use it," he laughed in his jocular way. But despite his laughter, I knew that he understood that my problem was an especially sensitive subject between Mr. Heifetz and me.

That night I was made painfully aware of how differently people perceive life! Upon arriving later at the "bash," another classmate approached me. "That is quite a way to get attention, you know," he smiled coyly.

Startled, I said, "What do you mean?"

"Well, you play the 'ingenuous' part very well."

I was surprised and embarrassed by his assessment of my honest feelings. Who else, I wondered, thought I had plotted to receive this kind of focus from Mr. Heifetz? I felt myself fill with rage. Obviously, I would have to learn not to reveal in words my personal trepidations. Besides, I reasoned, my teacher would always know my feelings anyway. From this point on, there is no doubt that Mr. Heifetz and I developed a silent understanding.

༄

The conflict between my life as a performing concert artist and my life as a student under the rigorous tutelage of Jascha Heifetz continued to plague me. How could I be ready for both things? It was a dilemma that I had to learn to live with. I had to find a way to be successful as both performer and student. I learned to "just do it" under any kind of circumstances. I recall, for instance, one Tuesday morning early in March before class when I was called to substitute for an ailing artist who would be unable to play a concert the coming Sunday afternoon in Palm Springs. I accepted. The first order of business in class that day was the assignment of the *22nd Caprice* of Paganini to be played by each person in the class the following Tuesday by memory. It was not an outrageous assignment, considering the pace we were all accustomed to. One week was a fair amount of time. However, I did not know this particular caprice, and it had never particularly interested me. Between Tuesday and Friday I was focused on what was expected of me for class on Friday—the Vieuxtemps *Concerto in A Minor*.

After class on Friday I spent that evening and Saturday in rehearsals with my pianist for my Sunday concert engagement, brushing up the program I had recently played in Emporia, Kansas, and Kansas City, Missouri. On Sunday morning my pianist and I traveled to Palm Springs to perform our afternoon concert at the Desert Museum. We returned to Los Angeles after nine that evening. Only then did I think of Paganini's *22nd Caprice*. When Mr. Heifetz had made the assignment on Tuesday, the following Tuesday had seemed a long time away. Now I was faced with the cruel realization that I had to prepare the Paganini in one day. Exhausted from performance and travel but ready to work, I proceeded to learn the caprice on Monday. After six hours of practice I was able to play it through at a moderate tempo. Only divine powers could know what might occur under the pressure of the moment the next day when I would have to play it by memory.

The class began on Tuesday with a surprise piano rendition of "Happy Birthday" in honor of my birthday, Wednesday, March 9. Oh, I thought, this is going to be far worse than I imagined. His expectations on my birthday will be crushed. Sitting in class seemed like a bad dream in which I listened to a series of superb renditions by other students, in particular the young Jacqueline Brand, while I wondered how I could possibly survive this. When it was my turn, I summoned all the courage and self-confidence I could muster and began to play. Surprisingly, with just one hesitation (Mr. Heifetz continued to tap the rhythm with his car antenna as I floundered for a couple of notes) I got to the end of it.

"What's the verdict, Sherry?" Mr. Heifetz asked.

"Guilty!" I responded.

"You know, Sherry, some people win friends and fame by being the best; others ..." He never finished. He needn't have.

# Sunday Afternoon Concerts

presents

### SHERRY KLOSS
Violinist

### AYKE AGUS
Pianist

## PALM SPRINGS DESERT MUSEUM

SUNDAY, MARCH 6, 1977

4:00 O'CLOCK

### PROGRAM

SONATA in G Minor . . . . . . . . . . . Tartini
    Andante
    Non troppo presto
    Largo: allegro con moto

SONATA (1949) . . . . . . . . . . . . G. Beglarian
    Moderato
    Adagio
    Allegro Scherzando

CAPRICE No. 20 . . . . . . . . . . Paganini-Kreisler

PRELUDIO from PARTITA No. III . . . . . Bach-Heifetz

SONATA in E Flat Major . . . . . . . . Beethoven
    Allegro con spirito
    Adagio con molt' espressione
    Rondo: allegro molto

ZEPHYR . . . . . . . . . . . . . . . Hubay

NOCTURNE in E Flat Major . . . . . Chopin-Sarasate

DANSE ESPAGNOLE . . . . . . . . de Falla-Kreisler

---

If you find it necessary to leave the concert, please do so between numbers and not during them. Performers appreciate your holding applause until each number is concluded.

This is the fifteenth season of Sunday Afternoon Concerts. There are to be seven programs — December 19, 1976. January 16; February 6; February 20; March 6; March 27; April 17, 1977. Supporting Patrons are listed on the over page.

Despite my juggling the rigors of being a performer and student, and despite my soul searching about "being ready," and despite the uncertainties of being a "freshman" in the demanding Heifetz Master Class, I survived the year. I better understood what was required in the class and learned a prodigious amount, not only about the music that lived behind the notes, but also about the way in which inspired teaching implores students to become their own best teachers. In a few short months Jascha Heifetz had changed my life, and his influence upon me had only just begun.

## The Second Year
(1975-76)

"You always get another chance . . .
that is, if you deserve it."

When I returned to Los Angeles for my second year with Mr. Heifetz, I moved into a little apartment above a garage in the historic Wilshire Ebell area. A very modest place, it had one large room with French windows, a separate tiny kitchen, and an even tinier bathroom with only a plastic drawstring curtain for a door. On a hot mid-August afternoon just after I had moved in, I was busy arranging the kitchen and unpacking my belongings while my wonderful Chinese landlord was putting the finishing touches on the fresh paint job. I was wearing only a scanty two-piece bathing suit. Perspiration glistened on my body and my hair was in a high ponytail to keep cool. I couldn't wait for cooler weather to arrive to get the apartment organized because I was anxious to get settled in my new place. Suddenly I heard Mr. Chu, my landlord, who was looking out the window, say, "Oh, I think your teacher here." Such a possibility seemed out of the question. I rushed to the window, and, sure enough, there was Mr. Heifetz getting out of a car. I grabbed the closest clothes I could find and dressed hurriedly. I must have looked frightful.

There were two raps on the door with his walking stick. When I opened the door, Mr. Heifetz said, "Hello, may I come in?" He wore a tweed sport jacket, dark trousers and a hat. The heat of that August day did not seem to touch him. He carried a cowhide L. L. Bean sack, which, I was to learn as I got to know him better, he took almost everywhere he went.

"Just wanted to visit your new home," he said, climbing the white-painted steps to the living room. "This is a housewarming, and I am the uninvited guest."

He reached into his sack and pulled out a bottle of wine. "This is for you. Housewarming!" he said as he reached again into his sack. "And this is for me," he said as he revealed a bottle of bourbon.

With his critical eye he scrutinized the faded, raggedy green carpet over linoleum flooring, the white metal table with painted red legs and matching hard metal chairs, the rust-colored paisley pull-out couch, and the jarringly bright orange curtains that I had made to adorn the French windows. I was prepared for a reaction of some kind to what he saw. Instead, while I was standing in amazement that Jascha Heifetz had taken the time from his life to appraise a student's living situation, I was further stunned when he asked, "What's for dinner?"

At long last it was his turn to swallow his surprise when I responded, "Spaghetti."

As we sat at that rickety red and white table and began to eat the "feast" (he asked for ketchup after the first taste), I realized that this legendary man was human beyond anything I had comprehended during my first uncertain year as a student and certainly beyond what the world knew about him.

That spaghetti dinner marked an odd and auspicious beginning to my second year with Jascha Heifetz. Although I was to remain awestruck by his profound artistry all my life, I was beginning to appreciate my new glimpse of who he was. Still, I was cautious even on informal occasions. It was not easy for me to adjust to this side of Mr. Heifetz. He was, after all, my teacher, the role model for whom I had enormous respect. I wanted to maintain this relationship whether we were in the classroom or in my own home.

One day early in that class year I got a call to join Mr. Heifetz, his personal secretary Annette Neblett, and Ayke Agus for a picnic in Hancock Park on the grounds of the Los Angeles County Museum of Art. Since Mr. Heifetz was providing the sandwiches, I decided to bring the drinks. It was a lovely warm day and the park was close to where I lived, so I chose to bicycle there. Because the invitation had been casual, I didn't give much thought to my dress. He was a stickler for adhering to a strict dress code in class: dresses, hose and heels for women, and suits and ties for men. Still, this was to be a picnic. So I wore biking clothes, including gloves and helmet. In my backpack I loaded soda, paper cups and, at the last minute, some freshly cut flowers and a vase for the centerpiece. As I approached the park, I laughed at my get-up, but I told myself, "This is a picnic."

When we met in Hancock Park, it was a wonder to see my teacher's idea of a picnic outfit. Noble as always, he was "poised," dressed fashionably in a sport jacket, sport trousers, a hat and very dark sunglasses, his idea of going out in public incognito. As usual, he carried his L. L. Bean leather sack. Despite his own smart look, he didn't seem to mind my "chic" biking gear.

We quickly found a shady spot for our blanket to the right of the museum and adjacent to the La Brea Tar Pits. Mr. Heifetz seemed to enjoy himself totally, taking note of the surroundings with great interest on this delightful day. The trees were in colorful and fragrant blossom, children played nearby, and the sounds of traffic on Wilshire Boulevard filtered into our special place. My flowers were propped up so as not to spill the replenished water that I had to find to replace that which had leaked out during the bike trip. After we got settled around the blanket, Mr. Heifetz examined my Raleigh "Competition" racing bike and wanted to know how all the gears functioned. He was intrigued by the water bottle and the little battery-powered lamp that I had attached to the rear of the frame. There was a special glint in his eye as he smiled at his discovery of this new dimension to his pupil. He enjoyed getting an updated version of bicycling and all the accoutrements surrounding it in the 1970s. He was always interested in new things, even though he resisted new "complicated" gadgets. When it was time to eat, I placed my floral centerpiece in the center of the blanket, and although the drinks had spilled a little during the biking, there was enough for everyone. We had a wonderful time, and I came to know another facet of Jascha Heifetz.

꒳

During my second year these occasional glimpses of Jascha Heifetz, the man, were an excellent counterpoint to the arduous tasks of learning set by Jascha Heifetz, the teacher. One of the most powerful lessons occurred after he assigned me the Brahms Concerto at the end of a Friday class. Though I had never studied the work, I was to play it for the class the following Tuesday. The work of my weekend was cut out for me. I arrived home from class exhausted from the intensity of the day's lessons and from the two bus rides to get from school to my apartment. I had never learned how to drive, and so bus rides were an unpleasant, time-consuming part of my life. After finding a cassette recording of the Brahms, I listened to it as I ate some hastily made dinner. Then I began my weekend of practicing to prepare for Tuesday.

For some reason Tuesday's class was to be held at Mr. Heifetz's studio, a Lloyd Wright construction built in 1947, located behind his home in Beverly Hills. The change of location added more uncertainty for me since I had to rely on public transportation to get there, and I was not familiar with the time schedule of that particular bus route. By Tuesday morning I had managed to learn the concerto well enough to get through it, but only just barely as far as I was concerned. I was extremely happy that I had not been called upon to step in for an ailing artist while I was preparing this assignment; so I was as "ready" as it was possible to be after three days.

Mr. Heifetz greeted the class and then looked at me. "Brahms?" he requested.

Ayke and I began the work while he listened intently through to the recapitulation of the first movement. Then he stood up and directed the "piano department" to begin at the top with the orchestral *tutti* as he began tapping the tempo of the theme as played by the winds and the orchestra.

"Now cut to the violin entrance," he directed as he tapped with his car antenna, not missing a beat.

I entered in the same tempo, sloshed through the rumblings of arpeggios and other material that lead to the shimmering theme and, sure enough, I was still in the tempo of the opening orchestral *tutti*. We continued like this, with him keeping the car antenna tempo, through the entire movement, stopping only for him to make a few suggestions or mark something in my music. As he masterfully outlined how the musical line forged forward with the rhythmic structure, I felt his forceful presence in the music drawing me along the harmonic road with intensity and direction. I remember saying to myself, "Why, of course, this is it!"

It suddenly seemed so obvious how to play this work— just the way Brahms wrote it. What a genius my teacher was! Many artists seem to make so much fuss about the rhythm with the string crossings in the opening material that by the time the theme arrives, the momentum of the music has been dissipated.

Mr. Heifetz remained at my side to the end of the movement, and then, looking at me with an almost gleeful grin, said, "Now go home and learn it!"

My head spun with the understanding of what had been revealed to me—without intrusion, without words, with no excessive demonstration. He played not one note; rather, he illuminated the musical intent of the structure by setting up the rhythmic foundations, thus allowing the cascading arpeggios to flow into the spiritually elevated, shimmering theme. For me, all roads led home.

☙

Another of Mr. Heifetz's "rituals" that became powerfully clear to me during my second year was his religious respect for the score. No matter what was being played, Mr. Heifetz always referred to the score. Regardless of how many times he had performed or recorded the violin literature, he still consulted the source. This habit of his was forcefully demonstrated one day when a student played the Bruch *Scottish Fantasy* in class, and there was a question about a note in the piano realization of the orchestral score. "Was it a C or a C-sharp?"

One student volunteered that "the recording has a C-sharp."

"Which recording has the C-sharp?" asked Mr. Heifetz.

"Your recording," replied the student.

"That may be. But what does the score say?"

Then, after looking at the piano realization and comparing it to the orchestral score, he saw the error, which very well could have been a misprint. He remarked, "I guess I have been playing a wrong note for many years." His droll observation was a reminder to the student that we must constantly re-check and then compare editions in order to get the most authentic understanding of what is written in the manuscript.

So I continued to learn more and more of the characteristics of Mr. Heifetz's complex personality: the strict, sometimes harsh, instructor; the organized planner of exciting lessons; the leveler of "fines" for musical and other infractions such as needing a haircut or using a plastic sack for music rather than a briefcase; the assignor of "itsy-bitsies" as special rewards; the caring mentor of those with problems; the uninvited dinner guest; the dignified dresser in sport coat and sunglasses; the lover of impromptu picnics; the devilish challenger who planned "surprises" in his lessons. But for me the most poignant aspect of our teacher's nature was his unrelenting concern for his students. He became involved in personal lives if he felt that it was necessary. He revealed this part of his personality to me on another occasion when I answered the phone in my apartment and heard Mr. Heifetz's voice.

"Ah ... hello ... it is beyond me," he started abruptly, "how a modern woman living in the 20th century has no desire to drive a car. And so ... well, what I am saying is, if you don't do something about that, you are out of my class."

I was stunned. "But, Mr. Heifetz, what does driving a car have to do with becoming a better violinist?"

Silence. A silence that implied that the question was not worthy of response!

I argued no further. I knew that he was right. I could only suppose that my arrival at the picnic on my bicycle had prompted this reaction. Had all his questions about my bicycle that day been some kind of subtle, or perhaps even mocking, hint that he disapproved of my mode of transportation? In any case, the die was cast. I had lived in Pittsburgh, New York, Boston and Europe, where public transportation was the norm, and, besides, I had never been able to afford a car. But now my violin teacher was expanding his influence into the world of driving. I got the message.

During the following weeks I found myself grinding the

gears of my girlfriend Marilyn's Audi as she taught me to drive. Mr. Heifetz was interested in every step of the process of my instruction. To him a student's development included much more than just progress on the violin. He was like a parent in his insistence that I become a more complete person. The day following my first disastrous driving test was a class day, and someone had informed Mr. Heifetz of my scheduled test. After class, when he asked about my driving, I had to tell him that I had failed the test. He told me to bring to our next class the paperwork that contained my ratings from the test. I felt like a child bringing my report card home. Showing him the results of that unfortunate test was the last thing in the world I would have dreamed of doing. I just couldn't expose my failure to someone whose opinion I valued so much. So, at the risk of incurring his disappointment in me once again, I decided not to honor his request.

In the middle of the next class, Mr. Heifetz looked at me with one of his riveting looks and said, "I believe that you have something for me today."

I shook my head "no."

He seemed bewildered but persevered and reworded his request more forcefully. "I believe that *I asked you* to bring something for me today. Isn't that so?"

"Yes," I said.

"And you have nothing for me?"

"No, I don't." I was fully aware that I might be asked to leave the class forever, but faced with the humiliation of showing my poor driving scores, I was prepared for the worst.

"Sherry, I would like to see you after class."

No one in the perplexed class understood what had transpired between us, but tension filled the air. I could hardly breathe and prayed that, in my shaky condition, I would not have to play that day. At the end of class, although the students found excuses to mill around so that they could satisfy their curiosity about the situation, Mr. Heifetz waited until they had all left before he questioned me once more. He seemed dumbfounded that I had understood what he asked for and yet had not complied with his request.

After a little more interrogation about my driving test, I felt my strength waning and tears forcing themselves into my eyes. "You know, Mr. Heifetz," I said with a trembling voice, "I am not very proud of the fact that I didn't pass the driving test."

His entire manner and tone of voice changed immediately. "Sweetie, I only wanted to help you. I couldn't imagine that you wouldn't pass the test, and I wanted to understand what you had done wrong so that I could help you. You will pass it the next time!"

Mr. Heifetz's touch to my driver's handbook.

And I did.

Once again I learned that beneath that brusque and sometimes stern manner, there was a sympathetic heart. I was slowly learning not only about Mr. Heifetz but also about the essential nature of good teachers everywhere. I made a mental note that should I become a teacher, I hoped that I would embrace some of Mr. Heifetz's qualities—the sympathetic heart, the firm hand, the unending interest in his students' welfare, and all those other quixotic traits that were a part of his genius.

↭

Mr. Heifetz's interest in his students' welfare extended, too, to matters of their personal appearance, probably because as performers we would need to be aware about such things. His students were clearly identifiable in grooming and presentation from all others who walked the corridors of the music building. In these matters he was sensitive to the sometimes fragile temperaments of the students, and so he chose most frequently to use a sense of humor combined with gentle cajoling to get his desired result. For instance, he offered overweight students twenty-five cents for every lost pound to encourage a diet, or to others he suggested contact lenses as an alternative to glasses. I recall one day when I had performed in class that Mr. Heifetz called me in for a private meeting after class. After everyone was gone, Mr. Heifetz closed the door and said, "You know, Sherry, when you are playing and really getting into it, you open your mouth. Do you have a problem with breathing through your nose?"

I was uncertain about how to react to this question, and so I looked at him cautiously.

"You know," he said, "if you don't keep your mouth closed, something might fly in!"

With that, the ice had been broken, and I laughed. He said the subject of breathing while playing reminded him of a time when he was performing in South America in terrible heat. The humidity was unbearable, and he was having trouble breathing. And as if that weren't enough, his violin had come apart at the seams because of the humidity, making it impossible for him to play it. He summoned a local musician to find out if there might be an instrument in the area he could borrow for the performance. A violin belonging to a local fireman was located and brought to him. All agreed to keep a pact of silence so that no one would know about the change of instrument. He did not want it to become the talk of the town. After the performance a woman approached him and said, "Maestro, your Stradivarius sounds marvelous." He responded with a noncommittal "thank you."

Mr. Heifetz smiled as he recalled the incident, while I silently chuckled with the knowledge that no matter what the quality of the violin, Jascha Heifetz still sounded like Jascha Heifetz. It was a valuable lesson. He rarely told a personal anecdote or allowed anyone to draw attention to "who he was," and when he did, it was just another way of preparing us for all kinds of eventualities in our own future careers.

On yet another occasion during that year, I became the subject of Mr. Heifetz's concern about personal appearance when he abruptly announced "lunch" and asked to speak with me in his greenroom.

Before class a group of us students congregated in the hallway outside the classroom had been amusing ourselves by laughing at one of our colleague's antics as he did an imitation of someone who had just stepped onto the elevator. By lunchtime I had entirely forgotten about my hysterical laughter. It was then that Mr. Heifetz called me into his room.

"What do you do, get dressed in the dark?" he bellowed.

I had no idea what was going on. "Yes," I answered innocently, "I don't like lights."

He continued harshly, "You know, you have plenty big eyes. You don't have to make them any bigger." And then he dismissed me.

It was all an enigma to me. I was mystified as I left the room, and it was not until I went to the ladies' room and looked in the mirror that I understood. Laughing so much before class had caused my mascara to run so that my eyes looked like huge spotlights surrounded by mud puddles. Belatedly embarrassed, I laughed as I wiped away the dark smears. I had just learned to be wary of the dangers of mascara that runs and to always check in a mirror before public appearances. Once again, Mr. Heifetz's concern for things other than music had taught me a valuable lesson.

༄

Later that year I returned to California from the wintry East wearing high leather boots. It was the fashion that year, and I, a tried-and-true Easterner, unconcerned by the change in climate, blithely wore them to class. As I prepared to play, Mr. Heifetz asked, "Are you still thawing out from your trip? Aren't galoshes usually slipped off of shoes and left at the door?" I would never have attempted to explain that these were not galoshes nor to argue the fashion of colder climates. After all, wasn't my teacher born into some of the most treacherous of winters? I got his message. I never wore boots to class again.

However, there was something I was wearing which greatly intrigued him. I proudly wore a new-fangled costume-jewelry-type of watch which my dad had given me for fun. It was a digital watch in a free-form shape, enclosed in a casing of blue plastic through which you could view all of the workings of the parts. When I forgot to take it off before playing, he noticed it immediately and asked me to remove it. I could see that he was dying to examine it, but, with his special sense of timing, waited until I started to play before walking over to my case, where I had placed it. He picked it up and appeared to be completely fascinated by it. "Digital or Digitalis? How many jewels?" He turned it over, looked through the back of it and studied it for a good five minutes. It seemed to me that he wished he had such a "neat" watch. I told him, "You may borrow it anytime you wish." The class gasped in shock at my offer, which, in my eyes, was simply a response to the honest, unpretentious curiosity of our teacher.

By the end of the second year in his class, I had become accustomed to the far-ranging interests of Mr. Heifetz. There was not a detail, either musical or personal, that eluded him. He "knew his customers" as he said, and he was determined to prepare us to face all the eventualities of life, musical and otherwise. Still, the future would hold many more episodes of unpredictability where he was concerned. He was an endless source of surprise.

೨೧

During the final class of each year we were told whether we would remain in class for the next year. We sweated out those last moments of the day wondering which names would be called for a private conference. At the end of the final class that second year, I was one of three students Mr. Heifetz wanted to see. As I waited nervously in the corridor for my turn (I was the last one to be called in), I watched as the first two students exited the room visibly upset. They said nothing to me and hurried from the building. I entered the greenroom with great apprehension.

Mr. Heifetz closed the door and began, "And you, too, if you don't pull yourself up by your bootstraps, you will be out of this class."

I knew he was serious. I could think of no appropriate

response except, "Are you not pleased with my work, Mr. Heifetz?"

"I want better work; I want more work," he replied. "You have the rest of your life to play concerts. You are here now to study. Schedule your concerts in the summertime when they will not conflict with class."

Like any great teacher, Mr. Heifetz demanded total commitment. Short of that, he made clear, you would be out of his class. He was totally dedicated to each student's progress while in class. I could not argue with that, and I left him that day much sobered but with a dilemma. My commitments to performance were not really a matter of personal choice, for I had won the competition before I had been admitted to his class. My prize contracted me to play concerts throughout the United States for the following two years, but I feared his unhappiness with my absences would linger. As I left that day, I vowed to work harder, but I feared that I might have to challenge Mr. Heifetz's rule about not performing. I would deal with that over the summer. The year was over, and along with the other students, I was feeling the great relief of getting successfully through another year with Mr. Heifetz.

# The Third Year
(1976-1977)

"You have to be convinced that whatever you are playing is the greatest piece in the world."

The challenge to Mr. Heifetz's interdiction against performing was to come, as I knew it would, during my third year. Early in the year I was presented the opportunity to do two radio broadcasts on KFAC Classical Radio in Los Angeles. With Mr. Heifetz's admonition echoing somewhere in my psyche I agreed to perform. The first broadcast, hosted by Harry Von Zell and Fred Crane, aired during the Christmas holidays. My tender pride forced me to adhere faithfully to my policy of not mentioning my performances to any of my classmates. I didn't want anyone to feel obligated to listen to me on the radio or attend a concert. So I was caught off guard when I attended the first class of 1977. After greeting the class with New Year's wishes, Mr. Heifetz turned to me and said, "You know, Sherry, you should have told everyone about the broadcast. You lost many people who would have listened. I just happened to hear it . . . all . . . every bit of it."

I could feel my face turn purple.

He continued, "I will talk to you about it at lunch."

At lunch he sampled one half of my homemade corned beef, and I tasted one half of his veal sandwich and stuffed chicken breast. As we ate, and as I waited with trepidation, he said, "You are one of the *lucky* people. Not only do you photograph well, you also record well: good sound, clear articulation, excellent control. Over all, it was very nice. Do you know what was the weakest?"

"Bach?" I ventured.

"No. When I mentioned to Ayke this morning on the way to school what I thought was the weakest, she missed a turn because she was so shocked."

Then I knew. Both Ayke and I had thought my best piece was the Ponce-Heifetz *Estrellita*, Jascha Heifetz's very first transcription in 1927 (he once told me that he "put everything but the kitchen sink into that one," referring to the wild harmonies). A little chagrined, I asked, "What was wrong? Was it too slow? Too boring?"

"No," he responded, "it was too earthy."

I didn't know how to respond, but I knew that any illusions I had about a "celestial" performance of that piece had just crash landed. Encouraged by his kind words, I felt better about having already accepted another performance date.

~

Each year class was canceled on February 2, Mr. Heifetz's birthday. Expecting this standard cancellation, I had agreed to do three performances straddling February 2: one in Houston, one in Rome, Georgia, and one in Nacogdoches, Texas. As the date approached, there was no mention either way about class cancellation. And, as I breathlessly awaited, there was still no word in class on the Friday that I was scheduled to depart. Not a word! I decided to risk it and departed for Houston and the Sunday afternoon museum concert. I felt certain that the reason he had not canceled class was to keep us sharp and working. Surely he would make the announcement at the last minute. Sunday evening I departed for Atlanta and arrived amidst a terrible snowstorm. I was greeted by my host's casual message that someone named Ayke had called from Los Angeles and asked that I return the call. When I did, the message was brief and fearsome: "There is class on Tuesday."

How dangerously I was living! I had known all along that if he didn't go away for his birthday, I would be "up a creek," and now it seemed I was, indeed, beginning that journey.

Was this snow a heavenly gift? Is that what all those snowflakes were about? I prayed that the snow would cause a cancellation of the concert. I was in a state of panic, knowing that I was surely in trouble if I didn't secure the help of an angel to fly me back to my orange, padded seat in the classroom by Tuesday at 11:00 a.m. But I awoke Monday morning to the newspaper article about my arrival, to a crisp and beautiful day, and to an anxious pianist waiting to rehearse. I needed to hold on to reality. There were to be no saving angels, and my concert was to go on. On Tuesday, February 2! Just as Mr. Heifetz celebrated his birthday on February 2 and class was in session February 2!

Early Tuesday morning I phoned Mr. Heifetz's assistant Yukiko Kamai. When she asked if I was ill, I answered, "No, it's just that I am not at home and will never be able to make it to class on time," struggling to stay as close to the outrageous truth as possible. I was a nervous wreck for the Rome concert, and then I flew back to Texas, to Nacogdoches, for my Thursday evening performance. I knew one thing for certain. Come Friday morning at 11:00. I would be sitting in my seat in the classroom, even if I had to walk. Weather in this little college town had not permitted early morning air departure for Dallas for three days because of fog. With this knowledge, I engaged two students to drive me to Dallas so that I could depart for Los Angeles and arrive by 9 a.m. (I later learned that our 5 a.m. road trip could have been avoided as the plane did fly that day.) I got to Los Angeles on time at 9 a.m. and was met by my girlfriend Marilyn, who zoomed me home in her Audi by 10:10 a.m. for pickup by another classmate, always punctual to a T, who drove me to class.

Why my ride was late on this morning of all mornings was beyond my comprehension. I had traveled virtually all week to get to the Friday class on time at 11:00 a.m. At last he arrived to pick me up and then seemed to bumble along ever so slowly on the way to class. I was beside myself! We were late! Never had this happened to anyone that I could remember. Class members knew better than to be late. Mr. Heifetz was not pleased, and though I knew I was already in hot water, I listened as he called my "driver" in at lunch. The door was not closed, and I heard the following:

"And why were you late this morning?"

I could have sworn that I let out a shriek of horror as I heard the reply, "Sherry was late when I picked her up." Deep inside I knew that my friend was fighting for his life in America because of visa problems. He couldn't afford to be dismissed from the program, but it was a cruel irony that all those desperate travel arrangements and all those miles I had traveled were for naught.

After lunch Mr. Heifetz looked at me and queried, "Sherry, any reason why you look so funereal today?"

My trademark dark circles under my eyes could not have looked worse than they did. After class I was asked to explain my Tuesday absence. As it turned out, Yukiko had held class without Mr. Heifetz. I replied, "Mr. Heifetz, if I tell you, you will be very unhappy with me. Must you know?"

And so I told the story. I thought it was a miracle that he did not banish me forever, but I never revealed the untruth spoken against me by my colleague. Did Mr. Heifetz somehow intuitively know the truth?

Such was life as a student of Jascha Heifetz.

I remember later asking Mr. Heifetz for advice about how to arrange the order of one of my concert programs. He responded with an acerbic question. "Is this two or three programs?" he asked and suggested omitting the Schoenberg *Fantasy*, which was a favorite of mine. When I asked why, he replied curtly, "You wanted an opinion!"

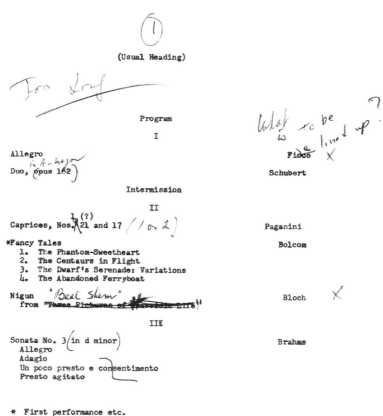

During the third year, the demands exacted upon the students became even more intense as there were just five members of the class. We had to be ready more often with always different varieties of repertoire.

---

**LOS ANGELES TIMES**

**Scholarships Available to study with Heifetz**

Violinist Jascha Heifetz and the USC School of Music have established the Heifetz Scholarship Awards.

Three full scholarships to study with Heifetz at the USC School of Music will be awarded to violinists with exceptional talent. Subsidies for living expenses will also be included.

Violinists from the United States and abroad may submit applications for consideration by Heifetz no later than Dec. 10. Applications may be obtained by writing to: Dean, School of Performing Arts, University of Southern California, Los Angeles, Calif. 90007.

Qualified applicants will be notified by mid-December to appear for auditions at USC's Ramo Hall of Music on Jan. 9, 10, and 11, 1978.

Heifetz will personally audition chosen finalists after a preliminary screening. The decision for awarding the scholarship rests solely with the maestro.

---

I knew then to the core of my being that I was in the presence of a great man, as I wrote my parents in a letter dated November, 1977. I had always known intellectually that Heifetz was a great man, but it was during this time that I internalized that understanding, that I truly "felt" that greatness. I continued to learn more about the man, his music and his unexpected, innovative ways of dealing with people and situations. By this time, I was one of the veterans of his class, and I was more able to have a proprietary interest in what went on. I was often called upon to perform tasks expected of veterans. Among these challenges was the job of helping Mr. Heifetz to fulfill social commitments where he felt the whole class was concerned. One such activity concerned Mr. Benjamin Rosen, the proprietor of Globe Music on Western Avenue in Los Angeles, who passed away in 1999 at the age of 104.

Mr. Rosen was a treasured resource for solving all quandaries involving music. A White Russian, he had been a pamphleteer during his youth when the Bolsheviks had come to power. Forced to leave the country with his family, he emigrated to New York and then moved to Los Angeles, where, as a young man, he worked mostly as a stage show violinist traveling with such stars as Victor Borge. He knew everything there was to know about music and had a scintillating personality. I recall one time when Mr. Heifetz was trying to identify a certain melody that kept running through his mind. Finally, unable to place it, he wrote out the melody on a tiny piece of manuscript paper and carried it around with him hoping for recall. At last, unable to solve the matter, he called Mr. Rosen, who identified the melody instantly. Because of such musical acumen and his special personality, he was a valuable asset to Mr. Heifetz and to the class.

One day Mr. Heifetz invited a few veteran members of the class to join him for lunch in the greenroom. After pulling out a supply of sandwiches prepared by his cook, he announced that the purpose of the gathering was to make suggestions about a thank-you gesture from the class to Mr. Rosen. It was decided that the most meaningful gift would be an invitation to visit the class. A few weeks later Claire Hodgkins, still Mr. Heifetz's assistant in the mid-1970s, chauffeured Mr. Rosen to class. Benji Rosen was "dressed to kill" in a suit from the 1920s, a colorful fancy tie, and a smile that burst with excitement.

After class had convened, Mr. Rosen was ushered into the room. Mr. Heifetz greeted him cordially and showed him to his special place to sit—the "guest" chair. I have never before or since witnessed a guest so honestly delighted. Throughout the class Mr. Heifetz, God-like to most violinists, and Mr. Rosen's hero of the violin, treated him with great respect and honor. At the conclusion of the class Mr. Rosen was presented with a basket of "goodies" that included fine Russian vodka and caviar along with a handwritten note from Mr. Heifetz. A photocopy of that note later was taped on the walls of Globe Music where it remained to his last day of business. Mr. Rosen recounted the story of his visit to the Heifetz class to all his customers time and again with the excitement of a child.

> To Mr. Rosen —
> In appreciation of his untiring resourcefulness for the cause of music-making —
> from the Heifetz Music Class —

Mr. Heifetz's regard for his colleagues was always respectful, just as his gesture to Mr. Rosen had been. When David Oistrakh died, for instance, Mr. Heifetz solemnly announced to the class, "I received a call from United Press International and was informed of the death of David Oistrakh. What a loss! He was so young! May I suggest that we all stand and observe a moment of silence in his honor." This esteem for other artists was a lesson in humility for the world-famous Mr. Heifetz to pass on to his students.

By the third year I had become accustomed to being in the presence of the great Heifetz and sometimes forgot how extraordinary my good fortune was. I needed an occasional reminder. I think, for instance, of the afternoon when my longtime friend and driving coach Marilyn phoned excitedly. "Hurry up . . . on Channel 5 . . . there's a movie with Mr. Heifetz and Walter Brennan . . . *They Shall Have Music.*" She hung up. I worked as quickly as I could to get a picture on the little set with a portable antenna that Marilyn's father-in-law had sent me from Northern California. (An unsolicited gift, as I am not a television viewer.) Then, before my eyes, there was Mr. Heifetz, in all his glory, saving a music school from closure by agreeing to perform in a benefit concert at the school with the students. My heart was pounding as I listened and watched. Suddenly I was reminded of how lucky I was to be where I was. I *know* him, I thought. He *knows* me. He has eaten my cooking. He *listens* to my music. He is *unbelievable.* He is *my* teacher. What more could I want? My insouciance faded quickly in the light of Mr. Heifetz's stardom. It was, as my Yiddish forbears might have said, *"beshert"* (meant to be)! There had to be a greater plan to my being chosen for the Heifetz class than sheer coincidence or my unplanned professional wanderings. I was convinced that some special providence had brought me to him.

༄

In lighter moments during that third year, Mr. Heifetz continued to reveal his sense of humor and his willingness to step down from the position of "world famous violinist." At the end of October I decided to have a costume party for Halloween and invited a few close friends, all the students in my class, and Mr. Heifetz to my garage apartment, where there was scant room for such a party. I was dressed as Tinkerbell, and my guests dressed in the usual cowgirl, dancing girl, clown, French chef, goblin and celebrity outfits, including a marvelous Groucho Marx. Mr. Heifetz arrived in a horrible, frightening rubber mask, but his identity provided no suspense. Propped above the curly gray wig he was wearing sat his familiar hat, and at his side he carried his trademark L. L. Bean cowhide sack.

We all knew who he was; however, he spoke not a word and he was terrifying to see. He approached me holding a small, round container. He motioned that I take it and turn the lid. When I did, a jumping jack lurched out at me. He had taken me completely by surprise with this child's prank, and I shrieked in astonishment. My loud and unexpected scream made everyone laugh and broke the ghoul's silence.

"Good even ... ing, everyone," he said, pleased with his performance.

Then he joined us as we gamed with Pin the Nose on the Pumpkin and bobbed for apples. Mr. Heifetz participated wholeheartedly, and we enjoyed having our esteemed teacher join in the fun of the ordinary, silly games. There is no question that we all felt closer to him after that evening. For me it revealed one additional dimension to the complex personality of Jascha Heifetz.

On another of these informal occasions I invited Mr. Heifetz and four other guests to dinner at my place. The main course included fresh salmon from Phil's Fish Market in Beverly Hills, assorted vegetables and salad. My homemade crepes suzette completed the meal. In traditional Russian fashion we "washed down" the meal with "down-the-hatch" shots of Count Michael's vodka (in the competition for best vodka, Mr. Heifetz railed against the very pricey brands). The meal went well, although Mr. Heifetz always said that I served too much food with too much starch.

Shortly before he left, Mr. Heifetz asked to speak with me in private. He led me to the farthest room of my apartment, closed the door, and then moved to the most distant corner of the room. Certainly, no one could overhear whatever it was he wished to speak to me about.

I waited.

"Sweetie," he began, "one day you may decide that you want to get married. You've got to do something about your cooking!"

I was speechless. I thought I had served a delicious meal.

Finally, I asked him what was wrong with the meal.

"My tummy will tell you tomorrow," he replied and then left the room to join the other guests.

As he was leaving, he said to me, "No, I don't have indigestion . . . yet."

I laughed, "But you have high hopes, don't you?"

He was enthralled only by my crepes suzette, and on my part it was only beginner's luck.

Months later Mr. Heifetz asked me to join him for dinner at his house . . . I was to cook the dinner. Tentative about my questionable qualifications as a cook and baffled by his request for more of my cooking, I assumed that *everyone* else he knew must have disappeared from the face of the earth for him to have requested me, but I accepted his invitation. When I arrived, he appeared visibly shaken because he had misplaced his keys—a very unlikely occurrence, I thought, in a man of such exactitude, and obviously a very unsettling situation for him. As I was throwing out some potato peelings while preparing the dinner, I glanced into the garbage container and saw his keys. My discovery enabled him to relax for dinner, but I was soon to learn that it did not moderate his critical nature.

When dinner was ready, I served the food at his place setting and poured his coffee into a large coffee mug I had found in the kitchen. Then I called to him. But he delayed coming to the table. I waited curiously, not knowing what to do. I did not feel comfortable calling him again as I knew he had heard me. However, while I waited, the food grew cold. When he finally came to the table, he took a bite of dinner, grimaced, and then said imperiously, "Fish shouldn't wait for me; I should wait for the fish."

Chastened for my misjudgment, I remained silent.

"And," he added, "coffee should be served in a demitasse."

Though he had been polite, I expected never again to be asked to step in as chef.

On two different occasions Mr. Heifetz asked me to bring my private students to his home so that he could observe my teaching. The first time, near the end of the third class year, I asked my student Janae if she would consider coming. A professional recreational therapist at UCLA, a passionate amateur musician, and a *great* sport, she agreed to present her work on my behalf even though she was terrified at the thought.

She arrived at his Beverly Hills home wearing a white dress decorated with musical notes. After introductions, he asked her a few questions about herself and then sat back for the show.

"Scales?" he asked.

"Oh, no!" she pouted, as she began playing with her back toward him. I played along with her because I thought that she would be more at ease that way. We finished the scale. He cleared his throat and said, *"someone's* out of tune. And . . . ah . . . would you mind turning around so that I can see you when you play?" He asked to hear the next selection.

"Janae would like to play the Mozart *Rondo,* something that she heard *someone* play on a recording," I offered.

He gestured for her to begin, and so she did—at about half the speed indicated. After giving her his full attention for longer than I ever expected, he cleared his throat again and asked rhetorically, "This person that you heard . . . did they play it at this tempo?"

My student had excellent instincts and realized that the interview was at an end. She knew that Jascha Heifetz had heard enough. She quipped with a giggle, "So, do you think I am ready for your class?"

Not missing a beat, he countered with a grin, "Well, it's not that you aren't ready for my class. It's that *I'm* not ready for you!"

Both of them enjoyed the experience, and I was pleased by the way in which Mr. Heifetz, by keeping the spirit light, infused a dignity into her quest for joy in music.

When my third year with Mr. Heifetz ended, I was more than ever aware of the effect his magical teaching was having upon me and of what a complex man he was. I felt more comfortable with Mr. Heifetz, the man, more prepared for his unpredictability. He always allowed me to be Sherry; in fact, he seemed to enjoy Sherry. Whatever critical reactions he had were simply indications that things needed attention and improvement.

# Summertime
(1977-1978)

"Let's hear the beginning and the end
... the middle happens."

On May 27, 1977, during the last class of the year, Mr. Heifetz asked all of us our plans for the summer. I didn't say anything. Finally, he questioned me. In a carefree manner I said that I was not sure yet, though I would be spending the summer in Los Angeles. Then came his loud booming voice, "You better be sure. You have a lot of work to do, and I will be checking on you." The class was taken aback by his unusual public display toward me.

I sent him a note occasionally during that summer to let him know how I was doing and that I was thinking of him. During August I received a call from him. "Are you free on Wednesday evening," he asked and then added, "for dinner? I will come to you."

Surprised that I was being asked to cook a meal again, I assured him that he would be welcome. I planned the menu and hoped for the best. About 6:30 on Wednesday evening, I was surprised to see Mr. Heifetz walking down Francis Avenue carrying his bulging cowhide bag. I never asked and he never did explain whether someone had dropped him off nearby or if he was just plain lost! But he was alone.

Before I could serve my own selections, he opened his cowhide bag and produced Russian delicacies including herring, crackers, egg salad sandwiches and vodka. He obviously was not about to take a chance on my bill of fare. So he hadn't forgotten my prior efforts as a cook! As we were enjoying his own Russian treats, he asked to hear what I was working on. Another of his "surprises"! No matter, he said, what stage of learning I was in, nor what the condition of the performance. Then I realized that the reason for this dinner was to "check" on my practicing. Despite the heat in my small, un-air-conditioned apartment, I played the Paganini *Caprice No. 23* and the first movement of the Bach *C Major Unaccompanied Sonata* and sweated all the way through the presentation. After offering some helpful suggestions about what I was doing, he left for the evening. I learned then that Mr. Heifetz keeps his word. He had come to monitor my work just as he had promised.

His summer visits were not always to monitor my work. During another summer, when all of Mr. Heifetz's friends and his secretary were away, I received a call from him and once again was surprised, for despite his rigorous insistence upon the formalities in class, there was that other side of him—the informal, often humorous. "How about we go to the movies?" he asked.

His invitation was well timed, for I had been wanting to see some old movies being shown at the Los Angeles County Museum, where I was a member. I quickly suggested this possibility, and after I had checked the schedule, we agreed to go see an old film entitled *My Man Godfrey* with William Powell and Carole Lombard, if, I added, he did not mind my girlfriend Muriel, visiting from out of town, joining us. Although I didn't mention it to him, she was in the throes of a difficult love relationship and had desperately needed to get away from St. Louis. I wouldn't have dreamed of springing a surprise on him by inviting a friend or enemy, no matter what the circumstances, without warning him first. He seemed comfortable with having her join us when he learned that she was a violinist in a major symphony orchestra conducted by Walter Susskind, with whom he had recorded.

When we met at the museum, it was already dark, but despite the darkness Mr. Heifetz, with his usual panache, was wearing a hat and scarf, dark sunglasses and carrying his walking stick. I assumed that his apparel on these occasions was designed to keep him incognito. Whatever his intention, his outfit, in addition to his physical presence, was bound to attract attention. After we met, he explained that "no one" was in town and that it was a relief to get away from the housekeeper. Mr. Heifetz refused the special senior citizen rate, treated us, and then led us briskly into the auditorium to find some good seats. Finally settled in his seat in the crowded auditorium, he removed his hat, placed his walking stick at his side and, removing his sunglasses, turned to discover Aniko, his housekeeper, just two rows directly behind him. It was her night off and she had decided to see the same movie. "Oh, no," he groaned softly, "I can't escape." I turned to see her, but she wisely kept her distance. After all, it was her night out, too.

And then there was poor Muriel! Sitting to the right of Mr. Heifetz and totally exhausted from jet lag, she kept nodding off throughout the movie. When the movie was over, Mr. Heifetz, with a twinkle in his eye, quipped to her, "We're not keeping you up are we?"

Flustered by his comment, she mumbled something incoherent and laughed it off. After all, she was not as accustomed as I was to Mr. Heifetz's sometimes stinging wit. And so the great Jascha Heifetz, the violinist's idol, would be remembered ever afterward as the man who interfered with her dreams.

During my years with Mr. Heifetz I learned that summertime phone calls, whether to check on my musical progress or just to escape the housekeeper, were to be expected. It was all part of the mercurial Mr. Heifetz.

# Sea Murmurs: At Malibu

"I ran out of medals."
To those who tried desperately to impress him.

When Mr. Heifetz felt the need to get away from the routine of his everyday life, he would "evaporate" and go to his favorite place—his beach retreat at Malibu. It was relaxing and casual there. He could be surrounded by magnificent beauty—the roar of the waves as they rolled in random patterns; the gracefulness of sandpipers, sea gulls and squawking blue jays; the aroma of moist salt air. Mr. Heifetz loved his beach home and often invited his friends to join him there. Guests were asked to arrive by 12:30 p.m. and would first be offered drinks while he personally enjoyed a gin and tonic. Then we would gather outdoors to watch the ocean, follow the boats along the horizon, view the activities of the members of the Malibu "Colony," and just talk while we basked in the relaxation of it all. I always enjoyed those occasions when I was among the guests.

The first time I was so honored was at an evening gathering at his home in Beverly Hills when he invited a few people to the beach for the following day. We were told to be at his home at 1520 Gilcrest Drive at 10 the next morning so that we could all leave together for the beach. There were three drivers, including Mr. Heifetz. After the other guests had climbed into their respective cars, Aniko, Mr. Heifetz's Hungarian cook, and I were left without a ride, so we were to ride with Mr. Heifetz himself.

After opening the garage door, he backed his gorgeous Bentley out of the garage. "How far we have come!" I reflected. Had I been about to go for a ride in his 1921 Model T Ford (his car of choice in that bygone era), my teacher would have been busy near the front of the hood cranking up the engine. I remembered his story of the special air horn on that Ford which blared the opening six notes of Beethoven's *Pastorale* Symphony, announcing his arrival to the country. "They always got advance notice," he said. I wondered as we sat in the driveway what special "extras" might accompany our ride to Malibu. Aniko quickly took the seat next to Mr. Heifetz while I was relieved to have my own generous space in the back seat of the beautiful silver and black Bentley, far away from my teacher. It was the first time I had driven with him.

As I had not yet learned to drive, I paid little attention to our route. I was just an innocent passenger leaving the driving to someone else. Mr. Heifetz maneuvered the car through the winding and narrow roads to Sunset Boulevard while I tried to keep my eyes on the road and get my bearings. I had no idea how we had arrived on Sunset Boulevard. Then the thrill ride began, and yet another aspect of my teacher revealed itself—Mr. Heifetz, the daredevil driver. He sped west on Sunset, zigzagging in and out of traffic. Or he meandered inexplicably for certain stretches. No one spoke during the ride, and I watched outside as this silver bullet swerved in and out of lanes on the Pacific Coast Highway, passing everything in sight. "Had my teacher been a racing car driver in another life?" I wondered. At times the ride became so frightening that my heart beat furiously and I wished I had stayed back at home.

Since I have learned to drive and have driven the road to the beach myself, I have confirmed for myself that my first ride to the beach with Mr. Heifetz had not been just a fast ride, it had been an electrifying, breathtaking, and scarily exhilarating experience, not unlike some of the musical feats for which the world remembers Jascha Heifetz.

One of the frequent pastimes on these Malibu occasions was Mr. Heifetz's favorite game of Ping-Pong. Before the usual beautiful lunch with varied menus of turkey, chicken, potato salad, corned beef or salami, Matjes herring and toasted bagels was served, his guests were invited to work up an appetite by playing the game with the host, who loved both singles and doubles. It was fun to watch distinguished people like Zvi Zeitlin, Grant Beglarian, Tamara Chapro, Jack Pfeiffer, or the accordionist Carl Fortina in the heat of a game with him. When not playing Ping-Pong, Carl often entertained by playing Mr. Heifetz's accordion, specially made with two keyboards instead of buttons. For his part, Mr. Heifetz enjoyed observing the various personalities and their behaviors during the games of Ping-Pong and learned more about the nature of his guests playing the game than they could have imagined. By the time lunch was served he had scrutinized the social dynamics that existed among his guests. And thus I discovered another aspect of the man: Mr. Heifetz, the acutely perceptive observer of people. Years later, as a teacher, I began to wonder if being a psychologist is not part of being a good teacher. If so, Mr. Heifetz practiced his analytical skills perhaps as much as he practiced his musical skill—both quite naturally.

Following Ping-Pong games, the loser was often "penalized" with an assignment to do some yard work around the beach house. Because I love yard work, I did not regard a trimming assignment as a penalty at all. In fact, I recall one time when no Ping-Pong losses were involved that Mr. Heifetz was doing some careful pruning with his handsaw to trim back his overgrown ficus tree. I had the best of intentions when I offered to "really take care of the tree." Surprisingly, he agreed and left me unsupervised to finish the job. I clipped away until

I was satisfied that the tree had been adequately pruned, and then, proud of my work, I settled back to enjoy the sea breeze. When Mr. Heifetz reappeared, he looked at the tree in shock, his eyes bugging out in disbelief. He lowered himself to the ground and lay on his back to look at what was left of the tree while I naively assumed that he was checking to see if I had done a thorough job. I soon learned that "thorough" was not the word he would have chosen for my handiwork.

"Sherry," he said harshly, "where is my ficus tree?"

"I gave it a crew cut," I replied.

He was not amused. He left instructions at the house that I was to be kept far way from the handsaw in the future, and he didn't let me forget that "job" for quite a while. But that was not the only time my destructive tendencies were costly for Mr. Heifetz.

There was also the holiday party for his students when my turn in the fun-filled Mexican Christmas game of the *piñata* cost Mr. Heifetz a new post for his teahouse. A brightly colored, candy-filled animal made of *papier mâché* was hung from the outside top rim of the teahouse under which the Ping-Pong table stood. We lined up for our turn at bat and then were blindfolded. Mr. Heifetz enjoyed being the one to carefully spin us around three times before sending us off with bat in hand. The challenge was to maintain equilibrium and direction in order to strike the *piñata* victoriously in just the right spot, causing the candies to tumble out. I headed down a perfect course as I listened to the teasing and heckling of the others. At the last instant I felt drawn toward the roar of the ocean and suddenly torqued my body and prepared to strike. With all my might I delivered the final blow. I felt the impact and heard a loud smash accompanied by the gasps and shrieks of the others. My blindfold was removed for me to see just where my "fine" sense of direction had led me. I had totally smashed in the center post of the teahouse. No one had *ever* done this. I was mortified and offered to repair the damage, realizing that once again my personal imprint had been made in an unflattering way.

Many times in the late afternoon Mr. Heifetz and his guests would leave the enclosed rear of the house (which he called the front because it was the side that faced the ocean) by ascending a few steps to a gate in the enclosed patio and then down a few more steps to reach the soft, sandy beach. Shoes were left in an orderly fashion on the steps. Properly dressed for beach protection, Mr. Heifetz wore a hat and sunglasses and carried his walking stick. *"Poidyum"* (Russian for "let's go"), he said. After that the walk was usually a silent one. It was a sensory experience to hear the rush of the waves and the cry of the seagulls as we scanned the imprints in the sand made by the sandpipers and other shore denizens like multicolored mollusks and scurrying crabs. We smelled the sea life forced by powerful Pacific currents onto the beach, tried to squash the bulbous pods of seaweed lying tangled in the sand, and stepped over sand castles built by busy children.

Sometimes on this private beach known as the playground of "The Colony," we would see a familiar Hollywood face. I was particularly impressed on the occasions when the movie stars approached my teacher with respect and admiration. They knew him for certain. Mr. Heifetz would be cordial but brief, seemingly reticent about receiving praise, as we would continue our walk past the homes of people like the Hallmark family, Rod Steiger, Charles Boyer and Lee Grant.

After about 45 minutes of brisk walking, during which time we might stop occasionally to sit on logs or toss sticks into the ocean or just rest, we would return to the beach house. Often in reversing our direction, we would have to fight the force of the wind blowing sand in our faces. At those times we welcomed spotting the teahouse in the distance. When we returned, Mr. Heifetz would enter the patio first in order to hand us a can of creosote to clean the tar from our feet. After washing our feet and stepping back into our sandals, we would come into the house where he would excuse himself for a "rest." He said good-bye to those who were not invited to stay for the evening and then quietly asked someone to knock on his door if he wasn't back downstairs by 6:30 p.m. I have sometimes heard guests claim that Mr. Heifetz disappeared at about 4 in the afternoon to "practice" for an hour while his guests were enjoying themselves. Those of us who stayed were free to walk some more on the beach, swim in the ocean, play cards, read from his wide selection of magazines (my favorite was *National Geographic*), take a shower to wash away the salt water, or just rest until the evening's festivities began. I especially remember one time when, just before going upstairs after four in the afternoon, he took out the piano part to the Wieniawski *Polonaise in D Major.* "We'll play this later," he said before he disappeared. I spent the next hour practicing the piano, fully aware that he would not make any tempo accommodations for me, the "pianist" of the day.

For the evening everyone dressed in evening wear—long dresses for the women and jackets for the men. When he reappeared, refreshed from his afternoon rest, his eyes sparkled and said mischievously, "And now the fun begins." He announced, "The bar is open," and we would be invited to join him. In the evening he liked Jim Beam bourbon. He always told me I was his "most expensive customer" because I enjoyed Grand Marnier. Then we would congregate in the teahouse outside and watch the sun set spectacularly over the ocean. Touched by the poignancy of what seemed like a divine message in the twilight, I hold those seconds among my most cherished memories.

෴

Over years of these evenings at Malibu I was introduced to

many of Mr. Heifetz's friends, his lawyer, his family, and his cooks Aniko and Maria. With this mixture of people Mr. Heifetz had already established long-standing relationships. His Russian friends called him Jascha, the others called him Jim— Jim Hoyle. At first I had no idea who Jim was and asked why they were referring to him this way. I learned that he had used this pseudonym for popular songs he had composed, including one called, "When You Make Love to Me, Don't Make Believe," recorded by Margaret Whiting. There were rumors about other humorous "recording projects" where, though the playing was intended to sound unbelievably bad, the person playing, Joseph Hague, yet another pseudonym, had to be unbelievably good to pull off such a stunt. At these types of gatherings, Mr. Heifetz encouraged me to call him Jim also. I just could not do it. He just was not Jim to me. He let it be. In time I became somewhat comfortable calling him Mr. H., as some referred to him. The evening's ritual was almost always the same. It began with the preparation for building a fire in the fireplace during the winter months. For this we would carry pine and oak logs from the front of the house where the wood was stored (the one that faced the road, but the one Mr. Heifetz called the rear) around to the rear (front). It was funny to see the women, sometimes very distinguished women in evening dress, wearing protective gloves and lugging firewood. An official fire person was always appointed and was responsible for keeping the fireplace alive. And the bar remained open so that guests could take their drinks outside to toast one another in the fresh ocean air.

At 7:45 we would hear a bell and then the Hungarian cook Aniko would announce in a heavy accent, "The dinner are served, Mr. Heifetz."

He never corrected her.

The cook served dinner formally. And the dinners were exquisite—Dungeness crab, Australian lobster tail, oxtail stew, bay shrimp on shredded lettuce, spraats, minute steaks or, one of Mr. Heifetz's favorites, chicken cutlets prepared with his own recipe. Usually, creamed spinach, potatoes and salad complemented the main course. On one occasion Aniko's successor, Maria, the Hungarian cook formerly employed by Zsa Zsa Gabor, made cream puffs for dessert. The guests loved them and complimented her profusely. On subsequent occasions we enjoyed hearty laughs as the dessert turned out to be cream puffs again and again and again. Coffee and dark chocolate followed the meal.

After dinner Mr. Heifetz, who thoroughly enjoyed these occasions, displayed his "common touch" again by immersing himself in delight with games of Charades, Twenty Questions, Yatzhee, Dominos, or card games like Gin at five or ten cents a point. He loved to silently analyze how his opponents thought out their moves in cards or Charades, and would throw his head back in laughter once he caught on to their strategy. One of my favorite games required listeners to identify works of music after hearing only two notes played on the piano. Often Mr. Heifetz encouraged people to offer extemporaneous renditions of music. He loved these games and so did I. Occasionally there was a night-cap of Marie Brizard (60 proof) or creme de menthe. As the time approached midnight, the guests departed for home.

I have long treasured my memories of the times I was included on those Malibu retreats. Each time my experience began just as soon as I left the Santa Monica Freeway and turned onto the Pacific Coast Highway. Ah, opening the windows, breathing the fresh sea air, allowing myself to be pulled into the rhythm of the ocean's roar, immersing myself in all the beguiling, sensuous qualities that made the beach so seductive! It was no wonder that Mr. Heifetz adored his Malibu house. It really was another world.

# Finale of the Student Years
(1978-1979)

"I occasionally play works by contemporary composers for two reasons. First, to discourage the composer from writing any more and, secondly, to remind myself how much I appreciate Beethoven."
—from LIFE Magazine, 28 July, 1961

By the time my years as a student in the Heifetz Class had passed, I had come to know the man as both stern taskmaster and intuitive parent. I had gained the confidence to take the initiative in demonstrating to my teacher that I did, indeed, think of him as a human being. He was now definitely not just a photo on a record jacket or a maestro sitting behind his desk in the classroom. In many small ways I came to appreciate the humanity of Jascha Heifetz because I was no longer too intimidated to make the kind of friendly gestures that my parents taught me to make toward friends.

Once when he mentioned that a cherished clock of his was not working any more, I offered to have my father, an expert watchmaker, repair it. After all, my dad had been trained in Europe by his own father, a clockmaker. If anyone could repair it, my dad could. Both parties enjoyed the challenge. Ben Kloss was excited to be working on this special little clock, and Mr. Heifetz was anxiously awaiting the outcome. Mr. H. never took anything for granted, and since all earlier attempts to repair the clock had failed, the jury was still out as far as he was concerned. It was April when the clock arrived in Los Angeles from Pittsburgh, ticking its heart out. Mr. Heifetz was pleased but slightly chagrined that he could find no bill in the package. He promptly wrote a note of thanks to Ben in Pittsburgh but stated that he wanted to pay for the clock. Otherwise, he said, he couldn't accept it. Ben had to give in to Mr. Heifetz's insistence.

1520 GILCREST DRIVE
BEVERLY HILLS, CALIFORNIA

April 14, 1978

Dear Klosses —

Thank you very much for your nice card with the good wishes for the Passover.

With warm greetings and all good wishes.

P. S. A special thanks to "Ben" for the clock (it is still running?) and much appreciated.

I had another opportunity to appreciate his humanness in simple things once when I had made some cheese blintzes. They were perfect, for I had followed my mother's recipe exactly. I took some of them with me to class the next day, not expecting to be invited to join my teacher for lunch. When I unpacked my blintzes, his eyes grew large. No question about it. He had a *big* interest in *my* lunch. Naturally, I shared my treat with him and watched as he tried one, slowly enjoying every bite of this traditional food and whatever memories it evoked for him. "Cold and fattening," he pronounced after devouring every bit, "and not bad ... not bad at all." If they gave him indigestion, he graciously never mentioned it, but on another occasion when I was on my way home from a party in the West Los Angeles area, I delivered a dessert for Mr. Heifetz and left it with the cook. The next morning I received a call from him. "Sherry, thank you very much for the package. I had your surprise with a tall glass of milk before I went to bed ... and ... I paid for it! I'm not supposed to eat glazed donuts, you know, though I like them very much. So please don't bring any more." I laughed at his mixed message of graciousness and bluntness. I got the message. No more greasy food for Mr. H. from me! Still, the experience made me understand him more.

Another time I risked presumptuousness by checking out from the magnificent Glendale library some books that I thought he might like to read. I went there often and gratefully appreciated the public library system. Although he had a large personal library, it occurred to me that he might like something beyond his own collection. He could not stifle his delight when I gave him the bag of books I had chosen. I could tell that he was anxious to examine the contents of the bag, but he wanted to do it in private.

"Well, thank you very much. When do you need to have these back?" he asked.

I knew that he hated to be rushed because he made that clear any time I presented him a potential concert program for his approval or disapproval. Not wanting to place any limitations on a potential source of joy for him, and not wanting to bother him with anything as mundane as due dates, I said, "Oh, whenever you are finished." I figured I would deal with due dates later.

I soon learned that there was no problem. If he was interested in a book, he finished it quickly. He returned the books promptly. So I continued bringing him books with a heavy concentration on Russian authors. Soon I lost track of what I had brought him each time. When I would arrive with a full bag of books, he would sift through them and gently remind me, "You brought this two weeks ago," or "I do believe that I returned this one to you *already.*" As he grew older and became less willing to make his forays into the world as he had always done so elegantly, my parcels of books became a way of bringing some of the outside world into his protected environment.

෴

As these years of coming to know him better drew to a close, he insisted, as he always had, on the highest standards and expectations for his students. The expectations in class were always boundless but embellished with humor. Asked to play a Paganini caprice one day, I decided on the *Caprice No. 1,* which I had aspired to master since I was nine years old. At that time my mother brought home the young Michael Rabin recording of the Paganini caprices along with the music. My head had spun as I listened to the unimaginable violinistic possibilities played by a virtual child—a genius child, granted. I was a rank beginner by comparison. I liked the *Caprice No. 1* very much and was determined to try it, but my small fingers could not make the stretches. However, as I and my fingers matured, I began to learn it. And now, twenty years later, I was about to have a lesson on it with Jascha Heifetz. I began the caprice with the spectacular ricochet bowing over the four strings outlining the chordal harmonies. From my point of view, I came much too quickly to the triplet thirds which demanded some time to be executed decently. Mr. Heifetz continued tapping the rhythm, and as I came to the end, I heard barnyard-like sounds emanating from the direction of the desk.

"Sherry, what is the tempo indication?" he asked.

I opened the music and realized that it said *Andante* (walking pace).

"Your tempo is too fast. The thirds sound like chickens clucking." As he continued to mimic my performance in chicken language, the class (myself included) laughed uproariously at his performance.

⁂

Among the most challenging of his expectations was playing chamber music with Mr. Heifetz himself. The times when he placed himself within a chamber music group were special moments for all, set apart from everything else in life. My heart raced wildly as I played, and I could hardly concentrate on my part let alone figure out "intellectually" what the beat was. So I always just went with the flow of the music. I would be so overcome by the sound, the direction of the phrases, the shadings of color and the power of musical interaction that I was transported to some other realm. When the music came to an end, Mr. Heifetz would smile with his eyes at all of us and then stand and say, "Thank you very much, one and all."

His words were not profound, but his sincerity was. He meant it. It was apparent to me that the music had affected him deeply, and he was truly thankful for the opportunity to give it life once more.

He showed supreme delight if a player did extraordinarily

well. Once, by the process of elimination because none of the other students wanted to sit in the first violin seat for a reading of a Haydn string quartet, I landed the "honor" of that seat. It turned out to be an extremely tricky and challenging part that required fingers to gallop all over the violin, particularly in the high register of the E-string. I was lucky and easily managed to negotiate all the technical traps involving fingering, shifts and intonation. There were some very nasty passages. Then Mr. Heifetz, standing directly behind me, asked me to repeat one of the most difficult passages. Certainly it was his devilishness which begged to discover if two times could be a charm. When it came to expectations, he was a master at raising the bar just a little higher. On the other hand, there were times when a student just "didn't get it" and the matter would be dropped for the time being. This occurred to me the time I played a Chopin mazurka. He listened, and when I finished, said, "Nyo, nyo, nyo . . . not really." He explained the characteristics of a mazurka, a dance. He demonstrated the steps, showing the lilt and the rhythm, and then he told me to think about it for the next time. Next time I tried again. And once again I heard, "Nyo, nyo, nyo. Sherry, this is not your piece. Maybe Fairy Princess (an allusion to my Halloween costume) should try something else. Next!" Another student volunteered to perform for him. Chastened by the wisdom of his judgment, I moved on to a different selection that could be "my piece."

In the summer of 1979 I performed at a music festival in Europe. On the way back to Los Angeles I stopped in Pittsburgh to visit my family and was greeted by my mother telling me that I had received a telephone call from Australia. I didn't know anyone in Australia. Baffled, I returned the call the next day and was offered a three-year university faculty position in Adelaide, South Australia. The school had gotten my name from the music festival in Switzerland, where I had been performing. Although it was clearly time for me to take this step in my professional career, I wanted to discuss the offer with Mr. Heifetz before accepting. I asked the chairman of the music department in Adelaide to contact me in Los Angeles the next week for my final answer.

When I returned to Los Angeles and told Mr. Heifetz about the offer, he asked me to bring the contract to his home in Beverly Hills, where he scanned the terms and listened to me describe the job and the location. He could tell that I was excited. After scrutinizing the papers for a while, he said with a degree of skepticism, "Well, I don't know about this Chatterton fellow, and if I know you, you will end up in Australia with a one-way ticket."

"Mr. Heifetz," I responded, amused at his lack of confidence in me, "if I do, well, then I'll just have to find a way back!"

I knew that I had to accept the position, even if it meant leaving the tutelage and close scrutiny of Jascha Heifetz, whose demanding expectations I had come to love. Mr. Heifetz also regretted losing me and my enthusiasm for the rigor of his teaching. In a letter to my parents dated January 1979, I wrote, "I am enjoying the classes, particularly knowing that this will be my last year. He asks me, 'Well, when are you leaving my class? It's up to you, you know. I don't like to keep anyone longer than I have to. It will probably be more painful for me than for you.'" I could sense that although he gave me his blessings, the goodbyes were as difficult for him as they were for me. I was to leave the womb-like life of his Master Class and go out into the world. It would not be easy, but I was sure that I would be the torchbearer of the Heifetz legacy while I was "down under" priming outstanding students for him, reviving memories of his unforgettable tours in the 1920s, and having the opportunity for my own career to blossom. Both he and I seemed to silently agree that I was "ready."

As I prepared to leave for my new life in Australia, I was filled with nostalgia. I could not help but think back to my early days with Mr. Heifetz and to the many wonderful things about being his student. I recalled how, at my very first audition for his class on that day in Malibu, he had mentioned that I needed a better violin. I was always grateful for whatever violin I played, but it had become apparent that I was now in need of a better instrument. Many of the violins I played during my youth in Pittsburgh had been offered to me as tokens of appreciation after I played concerts. Surprised and encouraged when listeners wanted to be involved in the development of my career by supporting me in this way, I always adapted with gratitude to whatever it was that I played upon. Often for important occasions my teachers had borrowed very fine instruments for me to play, and when I went off to New York to study at Juilliard, my parents bought at an auction two bows and a violin that Nathan Milstein believed was a Tyrolean or a Klotz instrument. It was this violin that I had brought to Los Angeles.

I continued using this instrument until March of 1978 when Mr. Heifetz noted that the neck and fingerboard had sunken and the distances were out of sync. He adamantly stressed, "There is no reason why you should have to suffer like this. Of course, one day you will have a much better instrument, but now you need something to play on." It needed some serious repair work! But when I took it to a violin shop for an estimate, I did nothing because I was unable to pay for the work that needed to be done. Besides, I was not convinced that I wanted to put additional money into this violin. I was ready for the next instrument in my life. Following that, on those occasions when Mr. Heifetz would "borrow" my violin to demonstrate a point during my lesson, he would note that nothing about the instrument had improved. Finally, he called me to his desk one day after class and told me to go to Mrs. Brown's violin shop, pick out three violins, and bring them to the next class. "And, uh . . . happy hunting." I followed his instructions. (I hadn't yet been "strongly encouraged" by him to learn to drive, so bringing the violins entailed carrying them on two different buses!) Midway through class Mr. Heifetz asked me to open the cases and give the instruments to a few students to play. He listened and asked for impressions and opinions. Everyone agreed on one instrument that was superior. Then he asked me to play the chosen instrument, and finally he asked that I bring the violin to him behind his desk.

Without looking inside at the label he carefully examined the craftsmanship and asked me if I liked the instrument. "I don't intend for this to be the violin of your lifetime," he said, "but it is a good, healthy violin." He offered a deal. "Trade you!" I gave him my Tyrolean violin and he purchased for me the Antonio Monzino. My "new" violin served me well through many concerts, and I used it in my first recorded album, *Forgotten Gems from the Heifetz Legacy.*

No. It would be impossible for me ever to forget the generosity of the "brusque and demanding" Mr. Heifetz. It was with these fond memories that I left for Australia.

# Encore: We Meet Again

"It's not the error,
it's the recovery that matters."
—referring to a breakdown during performance

My years in Australia were a joy. Mr. Heifetz corresponded during that time by leaving phone messages for me at the university (because of the time difference and the fact that I did not have a phone in my flat, I never did speak to him directly) as he continued to be a long-distance influence on my career. Then in May of 1980, two days after I had signed on to the university with a one-year contract extending my stay, I received a message which said, "Please call Mr. Heifetz before you sign any contract." I was invited to assume the position of his teaching assistant, a faculty position at the University of Southern California.

This created a major dilemma because I had just signed a formal contract and had cultivated an impressive class of pupils, some of whom traveled by air from Sidney and Melbourne for regular lessons. Apart from wrestling with all of the formalities of university commitments, I still had to consider that the Australian Broadcasting Corporation, which controlled *all* significant concerts in the country, was very interested in my work and had me busily and happily performing in recordings in Perth, *concerti* in Adelaide and Brisbane, and in various studio broadcast recitals. I was finally doing all that I had prepared myself to do. I was at long last a respected university professor and a performing artist.

However, I could not sleep! I knew that I was the perfect one to take on the role of Mr. Heifetz's assistant, and I feared that should I decide not to return, the class might dissolve. I would have to put my concert ambitions on further hold. And so I made an appointment with Dr. Gregor Ramsey, Director of the Adelaide College of Arts and Education, to present my situation. How sad those moments were! I explained that as much as I loved my position, my colleagues, the country and all the performing possibilities created for me, I felt an obligation to return. In a letter dated September 1980, I wrote to my parents, "My new position beckons me with challenge and rewards that only I can appreciate." I was offered more money, a violin, whatever I wanted. My response was simple: "Dr. Ramsey, this is not a monetary matter but rather a moral matter. I must return if the class is to continue. I owe it to his legacy." My departure was, indeed, difficult.

༄

I returned to the University of Southern California at a reduced salary to become Mr. Heifetz's assistant in his Master Class. In so doing I automatically became an associate professor at the university. During the next years I had the opportunity to see Jascha Heifetz from a totally different and illuminating perspective. Things that I had observed through the eyes of a student took on new meaning as I came to understand even better the magic of the Heifetz teaching. I came to understand, in a way I never had before, his commitment and responsibility where his students were concerned.

It was very important to Mr. Heifetz that his students have the proper environment in which to accomplish their work, and his charges were under constant scrutiny. As he had told me years before, "I know my customers." If he felt it was necessary, he would find ways to "quietly" help provide rent money, a new case, a bow, a violin, a "scholarship," an invitation to dinner at his home, a Thanksgiving day, or a Fourth of July celebration at the beach, so that no one was alone or lonely. I myself had been the beneficiary of this kind of generosity, but not until I was his assistant did I know how extensive his benevolence was. Beneath all his brusqueness and his sardonic wit, he was a caring and generous man. His commitment to excellence was unbounded.

His devotion to looking out for his students was also a lifetime commitment, and I continued to receive the benefit of his concern. I remember one day when I found among my mail a letter from the Harold Shaw Artist Management Agency in New York. All I knew about Harold Shaw was that Nathan Milstein and Andrés Segovia were represented by this impresario. I was pleasantly shocked to find a contract and a letter stating that Mr. Shaw had been trying to contact me by telephone for weeks and would like me to sign the enclosed contract as soon as possible. My head was reeling! Though I had communicated with a few possible managers, I hadn't dared to come close to the prestigious Harold Shaw. For a week I pondered what to do and finally called New York. I was immediately connected with Mr. Shaw.

"So, Sherry, tell me about yourself," he said.

It seems he had been at a world management conference in the Far East, and the Australians had been talking about the American violinist Sherry Kloss, so he sought me out. He wanted me to sign the contract quickly and return it in time for the publication of his new artist catalog. I paused at the thought of such a commitment. My pride insisted that he personally know what he was getting, and I asked him if I could show my work to him in person before signing a contract. At the same time, Mr. Heifetz made an appointment with his own attorney, Marvin Gross, to read through the contract while I was in New York. Obviously Mr. Heifetz's vast experience with managements, contracts and engagements for three-quarters of a century influenced the help he was giving me. Though Harold Shaw Management was the "cream of the cream," my teacher wanted me to be protected.

I flew to New York, engaged a pianist, and played for Mr. Shaw at Weill Hall. After my performance of Bruch's *Scottish Fantasy* and various "itsy-bitsies," he shook my hand and said, "You need a better fiddle. Now let us go to my office."

An impromptu meeting was called in one of the agent's cubicles with Mr. Shaw at the desk. I felt as if I were in the midst of strategic battle tactics of some sort. Full of excitement about impending concerts and relief that I would no longer have to personally "sell myself" to conductors and concert presenters, I sat back and observed the planning.

As obvious as it was for management to see the advantages of having Jascha Heifetz promote me, the artist to be sold, it was impossible for me to agree to ask Mr. Heifetz to grant interviews with me, for me, or about me. Nor could I ask him to act on my behalf to make calls to conductors. And to top it all off, I had to limit my availability to summer engagements because I did, after all, have a university position to honor and a demanding boss to satisfy. Absences during the school year would be impossible. Acknowledging to myself that I was not an easy client to work for, I, nevertheless, returned to Los Angeles with an elevated sense of self-esteem at having personally negotiated to my satisfaction a contract with Shaw Concerts.

Shortly after signing on with management, I was encouraged to make my London debut at Wigmore Hall. I thought about what type of program I wanted to present and consulted Mr. Heifetz. He considered my tentative ideas, and when I saw him the next time, he enthusiastically proposed the Howard Ferguson

*Sonata,* a work he had recorded with pianist Lillian Steuber, and the Cyril Scott "Tallahassee Suite." There was no question in my mind that the suggestion of English composers for my "coming out" concert was brilliant programming strategy.

Months later, with the date set and arrangements under way, he asked to speak with me after class. When all of the students had said their good-byes, he walked to the piano to put away his violin. He began speaking to me as if we had been in the midst of a discussion already. I heard him say, "So, you know that I have a Tononi?"

"Yes," I replied.

"Well, you know the Tononi, don't you?"

"No." I shook my head and said, "I have never seen it."

My feet froze to the ground as he continued, "Well, what I am trying to say—well—you can borrow the Tononi for the concert if you wish."

I was paralyzed, stunned, humbled, overjoyed and tongue-tied. *The Tononi violin?* The violin purchased by Ruvin Heifetz for his young son Jascha in Berlin! The violin my teacher, Jascha Heifetz, played in his New York Carnegie Hall debut in 1917! The one he had played in all of his early recordings! He stared at me with *those eyes,* and I could feel my heart thumping. Many moments passed before I was able to respond. "Oh, Mr. Heifetz, that would be unbelievable. Thank you!"

A look of satisfaction crossed his face.

After saying good-bye for the weekend, I left him in the studio and floated out to my car. My feet did not make contact with the earth and angelic wings delivered me home. My strength of spirit grew enormously after his offer.

As the concert approached, he told me that I could pick up the violin one week before departure. He asked only that I write up a letter of agreement. On the day of the pick up, as we transferred the Tononi from his case to my own, I was overcome by a powerful realization. Imagine what was occurring! He was providing me with the opportunity to introduce myself in a major concert debut with his own violin, the very instrument he played when he made his momentous Carnegie Hall debut in 1917. Now I *truly* had a legacy to uphold.

*Feb 16, 1985*

*Received from Mr. Jascha Heifetz: Carlo Tononi Violin and Vuillaume Bow on loan to me To be returned approximately March 18, 1985.*
*S.K. May 21, 1985*

*Sherry Kloss*
*3215½ Rowena Ave*
*Los Angeles, Ca.*
*90027*

The concert was a success with a very responsive audience of well-known and curious personalities (including the harmonica virtuoso Larry Adler) anxious to glimpse and hear the playing of one currently associated with the great Heifetz. The review was excellent, so I returned to California with a sense of accomplishment. In the studio once more to return the violin, we engaged in the reverse "ritual" of transferring the violin from my case to his own. He examined the instrument carefully and then closed the case. "Well, how do you like it?" he asked, turning to face me. I heard fiery resolve in the timbre of my voice when I answered, "Mr. Heifetz, I love the violin, and—I want you to know that should the time ever come when you desire to sell it, I would like to purchase it." I really meant what I said and felt that whatever it took, I would find a way. Again, he radiated satisfaction when he replied simply, "You will be the first to know."

His words still resound within my heart and soul to this day.

*Feb 22. 1986*

*Received from Mr. Jascha Heifetz: one Tononi violin and one Vuillaume Bow on loan to me; to be returned March 3. 1986.*

*Sherry Kloss*
*55 Pompadour Dr.*
*Ashland, Oregon*
*97520*
*(503) 482-1728*

*Received on March 30ᵗʰ, '86 (Easter Sunday) –*
*J.H.*

As assistant to Mr. Heifetz I sometimes acted as intermediary between him and his students. It required an understanding of the man's temperament and a knowledge that beneath his occasionally intimidating exterior, he was usually a reasonable listener where real talent was concerned. Once during my tenure as assistant I received a letter, tape and application from a violinist in Ohio. The tape contained some outstanding playing of the Paganini *Concerto*. The letter was written in perfect English, but it explained that the writer was on a visitor's visa from China and that she had dreamed for years while living in China of studying with Jascha Heifetz. She said that by the following year she would have had enough time to save the money to fly to Los Angeles to audition if she were invited. Sando Xia (Shia), visiting scholar at Kent State University in Ohio, had seen a flier advertising the Heifetz class on a bulletin board in May of 1981.

I called her immediately and invited her to come to Los Angeles as soon as possible because I needed to hear her personally. I knew that if she turned out to be as talented as her tape had promised, there was a good chance that Mr. Heifetz would accept her as a student. When she arrived in September of 1981, I learned to my horror that she spoke virtually no English, but she played the violin exceptionally well. I forged on and telephoned Mr. Heifetz to inform him that there was someone I wanted him to hear. He told me he was not ready to hold an audition as he had been traveling, and he said firmly, "I am not unpacked yet." By this time the potential student, Sando Xia, had patiently spent several days in a seedy Los Angeles motel room while I, knowing that she was nervous in anticipation of the audition and concerned about missing a $15 concert commitment back in Ohio, made more phone calls to Mr. Heifetz. Either he was unavailable, or he was just "not ready." I understood that as an older person he was probably fatigued from his travel. I bided my time. My next call to him, however, was forceful. I did not allow him to speak after he came on the line. "Mr. Heifetz," I offered, "you may lose one of the very best students that has come along in a while."

*"Don't push me,"* he responded with equal force and hung up.

I was baffled by what I thought to be unnecessary prolonging of the process. Of course, I was privy to all of the painful and nerve-wracking details of the student's situation, which he was unaware of and not interested in. True to his mercurial way, however, within a few hours my phone rang.

"Um—okay, I am ready. Bring her to the beach."

As I hung up the phone, the satisfaction which I initially felt in acquiring an audition time was replaced with a sense of terror. "When he finds out that she doesn't speak English," I thought, "he is going to kill me."

How would she fit into his fast-paced and high-powered classes? How could he accommodate her at his age? By this time he was in his early eighties and set in his ways. To ask for the patience required to deal with a serious language barrier seemed too much to expect. He was fluent in Russian, French, Hebrew, German and Spanish (which he continued studying two days a week). His international students refreshed his skills in Dutch, Japanese, Korean, Swedish and Finnish. But Chinese? I wondered if I was being fair to him by inviting someone who could not even say, "How are you? I will play the Paganini *Concerto.*" And how would he react to what I had done?

After her audition, despite my concerns, he accepted her even though she was in her early thirties. Ordinarily he considered a student "flexible" enough for learning only under the age of twenty-five. What I witnessed as he taught her was some of the best teaching I have ever seen despite the fact that verbal communication between teacher and student was impossible in the beginning. Mr. Heifetz demonstrated his examples even more carefully. He exaggerated colors, phrasing and style without using words. His innovative resourcefulness found the pathways to provide the education he thought she deserved. As I watched his patience in the face of frustration and his delight when he was successful in transmitting his message to her in tones, my already high opinion of Jascha Heifetz grew exponentially. I hadn't thought that it was possible, but this great teacher, even as an octogenarian, got greater and greater.

※

Shortly after my return from Australia, two of my Australian pupils also arrived in Los Angeles to continue private study with me. Both young men were sixteen years old. Our work for the upcoming year was directed toward *the* audition for the Heifetz class. Jonathon, from Adelaide, was of European descent, and Yuki, from Melbourne, was Japanese. Their personalities were diametrically opposed.

When I was asked once again to bring my students to "the house" for Mr. Heifetz's observation, it was natural that these two would be the ones I chose. We arrived together and were buzzed into the side entrance which led to the teaching studio. Both young men were dressed in their best attire, Jonathon in his tweeds and a collarless shirt with waistcoat, Yuki in a Gucci outfit. Their shoes were shined, and they were cleanly shaved and perfectly groomed. I had given strict instructions about their personal appearance. Scales as well as pieces by Bach, Brahms, Paganini and Kreisler had been prepared, and the audition had been diligently rehearsed. This would truly be a test of my efforts, reflecting more than two years of work.

With all the important staples of the Heifetz regimen in healthy order, I was confident that each one of the young men would project his particular talent and show the reason why I chose to devote my time to them. I was not prepared, however, for their honest—though understandable—demonstration of awe and innocence at meeting Mr. Heifetz. After being introduced to him at the door of the studio, Jonathon froze. He became a statue blocking the doorway. Mr. Heifetz could not get past him and asked, "Mind if I come in?" Yuki entered the studio, looked around, and offhandedly burst out with, "Nice place you have here!" Although I knew the aberrant reaction of both students was simply due to nerves, I slithered to my chair wondering what other surprises might be in store for me once they began to play. But, happily, both of their musical presentations filled me with tremendous pride. I felt confident that in a short period of time they would be ready for the formal class audition.

Mr. Heifetz carefully and tactfully assessed the progress they were making with me as their teacher. He was gentle in his remarks to the performers. Clearly, this was *my* audition. Afterward, he wished them much luck in life and then asked to speak with me in private. After making some predictably succinct observations, he agreed with my own judgment about the talent of these students, and as a final comment offered, "One of them is overdressed and the other is underdressed." Then he bade us farewell and waved good-bye as we left. Once again the reigning 20th century legend of the violin demonstrated humility and a generosity of spirit. Showing an interest in these students would serve as an inspiration in their lives. With a sense of elation we piled into my Toyota and rolled down the hill from the home of the master.

༃

The following year three guests from China visited Heifetz's class. All women—two from Shanghai and one from Beijing—they were thrilled to have an audience with Jascha Heifetz. One of them, Ms. Yu li-na, a very tall and attractive violinist, had a substantial career in China, where she had achieved fame for her recording of "Butterfly Lovers Violin Concerto" (Liang Shanpo and Zhu Yingtai) composed by Gang Chen. I marveled at the way in which Mr. Heifetz carried on the class routine, finding ways to include the guests. If something needed translation from either English or Chinese, Sando Xia, whose command of English had by this time improved, acted as interpreter for everyone. When they departed, they gave Mr. Heifetz some gifts, including the violin/piano score and tape of the "Butterfly" concerto. I was intrigued and looked forward anxiously to hearing a Chinese violin concerto.

A few classes later Mr. Heifetz asked if anyone would be interested in listening to the recording. When I raised my hand, he lent me the tape. I absolutely loved hearing the work, but subconsciously I knew that I would never be able to play in the distinctive style that characterizes the Chinese sound. However, out of curiosity I wanted to look at the score and further confirm my "gut feeling." For the next class, when I returned the tape, I asked Mr. Heifetz if I might have the music to the concerto.

He looked straight at me and said, "No."

I was very surprised and wondered why not, but I let it alone. At the next class he asked Sando to perform the "Butterfly" concerto. I looked forward to hearing her play it, and as she played, I felt her capture the essence of the piece, using the traditional Chinese sliding sounds which seemed to overflow one into the other with just the perfect timbre and tone coloring. There was a spirit and naturalness that just happened. How magical it seemed that in the Beverly Hills studio, high above the city of Los Angeles, it was music that bridged the gap created by geography and politics! The room was filled with sounds that emanated from her heart and soul, her upbringing and culture. It was so *right!*

When she finished, Mr. Heifetz tossed his pencil down on his desk and said with pride and conviction, "Now, she (Ms. Yu li-na) is not the only one to play this piece." I realized then that in refusing me the music, he had been giving me another message. This concerto was not for me, coming from a Polish-American upbringing. It clearly belonged to the culture of the Far East.

1520 GILCREST DRIVE
BEVERLY HILLS, CALIFORNIA

November 22, 1983

To Whom It May Concern:

This is to confirm that San-Do Xia is an active student in my violin class.

San-Do is extremely talented and making excellent progress. She is very important to my class and is on a partial scholarship so that she may continue. It is my feeling that she is serious and ambitious regarding her violin studies.

Jascha Heifetz

# Gifts

"Utilize, don't analyze."

When I returned from my professional life in Australia, I could afford to move from my little garage apartment to larger, more respectable accommodations. After finding a beautiful one-bedroom apartment in the Los Feliz area near Griffith Park, I gradually began to furnish the space. I had only just begun my decorating, and the rooms were sparsely appointed, when Mr. Heifetz arrived one day for a visit. He seemed pleased and carefully investigated the entire apartment amidst unpacked boxes, housewarming gifts, and lots of junk collected from my earlier gypsy years. After a while I noticed that he was pacing back and forth in the living room. He seemed to be measuring the space silently. I did not inquire about his focused mission. I just thought he was trying to imagine whether or not a string quartet could fit into the living room.

When he noticed a rolled-up tapestry among my gifts, he asked, "May I?"

I nodded consent, and he unrolled the piece, examining for quite some time the colorful scene of a Renaissance musical gathering.

"Charming," he said. "Do you have a hammer and nails?"

When I produced the tools, I watched as he hung my tapestry on the wall in the place that he thought was appropriate. I never changed its placement because, as the apartment took shape over the next several months, it turned out that his instinctive sense of the right location for the piece was perfect. One more facet of his amazing personality—Jascha Heifetz, the interior decorator!

A few weeks later I received a delivery of carpet for the living room. As I signed the receipt for this 7x9 foot roll of carpet, I couldn't help but notice that this "house-warming" gift had cost a hefty $460. Perfect size! Perfect color! Then I understood why he had paced out the living room during his first visit. I was still to be the beneficiary of his generous spirit.

And yet another gift to that apartment was the Knight piano that had been in his greenroom at school. When he severed the relationship with the University of Southern California in 1985, as a result of a change of administration which demonstrated a lack of respect and understanding for the institution of the Heifetz Class, he called me and asked that I have it removed. I asked, "Where do you want it to go?" and he replied, "Your apartment." I was stunned but overjoyed. The piano had become an important part of my musical life, and I truly missed not having one of my own. From that time on, when Mr. Heifetz visited or came to dinner, the piano was the focal point of the visit. He would take out a pile of music from his L. L. Bean bag and sit at the piano. This was the cue that I was to get out my violin so that we could read through the music together. I recall Albert Spalding's *Etchings* among the music that I did not know. Years later I included it on one of my recordings.

༄

Although he enjoyed giving gifts, he was reluctant to accept them. I recall one time on tour in the Midwest when I was invited to the home of a lovely elderly couple. The gentleman was a retired railroad man whose passion at the age of eighty was woodworking. Among his handicrafts was an exquisite music stand he had carved for his wife, who was a flutist. When I commented on the beauty of the piece, he excitedly invited me to the basement to see his "art pieces." As I surveyed his work, I was particularly taken by some little violin-shaped stools that he had made from various beautiful hardwoods: maple, oak, cherry, birch. I quickly figured out how many of these little pieces I could manage to carry back to Los Angeles, and I bought them then and there.

Shortly after I had returned home, when I was invited to Mr. Heifetz's home for dinner, I arrived with one of the precious little stools, which I thought would fit perfectly under the coffee table in his living room. It could be pulled out, I thought, when someone wanted to sit at the other end of the couch for an intimate conversation. The housekeeper Maria led me into the house, where I quietly went into the living room and placed my gift near the coffee table before Mr. Heifetz came in. After he had entered and greeted me, we sat down to visit.

"Anyone follow you? Any fish stories?" he twinkled, anticipating my usual unbelievable adventures. He continued, "Now, I want everyone to know that these stories Sherry tells us couldn't possibly happen to anyone else. Well, yes, there is an exception. Her mother. They sometimes happen to her mother, too."

I laughed as I remembered the story I had once shared with him about my mother walking home from shopping in the middle of the winter. Suddenly she spied a large fish lying in the snow. She picked it up, brought it home, and served it as part of a beautiful lunch.

Anticipating one of my good stories, he suddenly noticed the stool.

"Where did this come from?" he asked.

After I told him the story, he studied the piece carefully for the rest of the evening, and as I said good night, he handed me the violin stool.

"Thank you," he said, "but you should take that home with you."

On the other hand, the tie which my parents had sent along with me for him received a different response: "Just the right width, lovely color. Please thank Ben, Myrna and Herb, and send regards for me, will you?"

Forever the unpredictable Heifetz! I was not offended but rather disappointed by his reluctance about accepting my gift, and since one of the other guests that evening had desperately wanted the stool, it found a good home. Only the tie scored a win!

⌘

One unusually hot September day, when the Santa Ana winds were searing Southern California, I had to drive to the San Fernando Valley to pick up my Monzino from Hans Benning, luthier of Studio City Music Shop, where it was being repaired. By this point in my career I had become frustrated with the Monzino and was ready for another instrument, but I could not yet afford to replace it. During the return trip to my apartment I was suffering so much from the heat that I felt I could not continue until I immersed myself in the cool waters of the Pacific, and so I quickly changed directions and headed for the beach. Worried about the safety of my violin, I parked in the attended lot. Then I placed the instrument in the trunk, hid it under some blankets, took my bathing suit out of the trunk and, after a quick change, ran into the ocean to escape the affliction of the heat.

When I returned only about fifteen minutes later and opened the trunk to deposit my swim suit, I realized the car had been broken into. Everything was gone!

My heat affliction was replaced by a wave of temporary insanity. I was hysterical. How could I have been so stupid? What was I to do for an instrument? And how could I ever explain to Mr. Heifetz what had happened? In a state of total hysteria I drove to the Santa Monica police station to report the theft. As I drove home, sweltering, I felt utter despair. The worst feeling of all was the emptiness at having lost the violin, which had been an important gesture of validation from Jascha Heifetz.

I kept my despair to myself for two days until I could summon the courage to call and inform him of the occurrence. "Mr. Heifetz, I need to talk to you," I said with urgency. "Come to the beach on Saturday," he replied. The two-day wait was hell, and I arrived at the beach that Saturday totally filled with anxiety. Mr. Heifetz's son Jay, daughter-in-law Louise, and their newborn child Anna were among the guests that greeted each other that day. I patiently waited while Mr. Heifetz held his granddaughter and shared special time with his family. While all of the beach activity continued—refreshments, lunch, Ping-Pong, visiting, laughing, teasing—I could feel my physical and emotional strength dissipating. That I had driven those miles from Los Feliz to Malibu was a minor miracle to me. The previous few days were lost in my mental fog. I was a wreck! Eventually he turned to me and said, "I believe you wanted to speak with me?"

He led me to a secluded spot near the Ping-Pong table and motioned for me to sit down. I had his full attention. His huge eyes peered at me.

"Mr. Heifetz," I said, "something terrible has happened." I gulped, feeling full of guilt about my carelessness, thoughtlessness and foolishness. My heart was pounding in my ears and drowning out the waves breaking just behind us. I wondered if he could hear my heart. "The violin you gave me has been stolen."

He was silent for a long, long while. At last he said, "Most often these things are caused by carelessness."

That was all he said. He didn't ask for any details about how the violin had been stolen so that I did not have to explain my stupidity. I felt enormous gratitude for his understanding of my pain. Once he knew the violin was gone, there was little else that either of us could say. Before I left the beach that day, he offered to lend me his "beach" violin and bow. I was overwhelmed by this gesture, but I could not bring myself to accept.

Upon learning what had happened, my friend Glen said, "Sherry, this is the best thing that could have happened to you. Now you can add a little to the insurance payment and get yourself another violin." In the meantime I was offered the use of a nice violin belonging to my student.

About three weeks later, I received a phone call from a Detective Oswald of the Santa Monica Police. "Sherry, I have a violin I'd like you to look at," he said.

"Is it mine?" I cried.

"Can't say for sure. You've gotta come on over here."

I raced to Santa Monica. When I arrived on the second floor of the precinct station, I saw a group of police hovering around a desk belonging to the detective. I stormed the area and screamed as I recognized my case—missing its cover. I quickly opened the case and discovered my dear violin and all its equipment in perfect condition—the violin still perfectly tuned with no sign of trauma. As it turned out, the only damage that had been done was the result of the thief's attempt to camouflage the appearance of the stolen goods by stripping the case of its outer canvas covering. Lying honestly beneath the lid of one of the small compartments was the receipt from Studio City Music for the work done. It had my name on it and was dated with the day I had picked up the instrument. There was no question whose violin it was! It was mine, my dear Monzino, the gift from my teacher Jascha Heifetz, hocked for a mere $65. It would be impossible to describe my relief at putting my hands on that violin once more. Everybody there cheered and applauded this reunion. Only then did Officer Oswald confess his particular interest in the case when he told me that he had studied violin as a child.

I *happily* returned home, *gladly* returned the insurance check which I had just received the previous day, and *devilishly* put in a call to Mr. Heifetz to tell him the good news. When I later told him the whole story with all the details, he shook his head in disbelief that I had been so lucky, silently communicating "Only Sherry!" (He was probably thinking "another fish story.") My suffering had been relieved.

∽

As the Jewish New Year approached, I received an invitation to break the 24-hour Yom Kippur fast with Mr. Heifetz at his Beverly Hills home. I did not know the extent of my teacher's personal religious practices, other than having received an expression of thanks for my family's holiday cards to him. I decided to bake the traditional round holiday challah for the occasion. With two other guests, we sat in the enclosed porch at a little card table where Mr. Heifetz often ate his lunch. The table was already set for tea. A small bowl of honey and a cut-up apple were placed in the center of the table. Overlooking all of Los Angeles from this spot, we waited for the sun to set, signaling the end of the fast. I was anxious to discover how much, or even if, Mr. Heifetz would participate in the rituals of this holy day of atonement. We listened to the soulful sounds of the shofar being blown by one of the guests; we recited the blessings over the challah and apple, dipping each piece into the bowl of honey to signify the beginning of a new and sweet year. There was no prompting necessary. Mr. Heifetz was very much the willing and knowing participant. As he fumbled to maintain the position of his yarmulke, the skullcap worn by Jews for religious occasions, I wondered about his personal religious training in the Russia of the tsars during the early 1900s. I imagined that his particularly beautiful velvet skullcap must have had a story behind it that I longed to know but was too shy to ask. There was a deeply serious and respectful manner about the way in which he embraced these rituals. The poignant sense of intimacy in a shared history passed on from generation to generation was yet another bond in our relationship.

# Lifelong Friendship

"Hello, hello, hello."

Over the years my relationship with Mr. Heifetz grew to include, besides music, a personal rapport that I prized. Eventually I considered myself to be a member of his wide circle of friends, though I continued to think of myself as just Sherry, yes, the sometimes unpredictable Sherry, a pupil of Jascha Heifetz. I was often invited to join his group on social occasions. It was sometimes a gathering in Palm Springs with all accommodations arranged in a private home. These occasions provided a joy of sharing and being together in the privacy of another person's home—a cozy family feeling. There was a true sense of holiday reflected in the casual dress and the unstructured timing of meals that was unlike the flow of a day at Malibu. Perhaps there would be a card game going on in one corner while others swam, played tennis, or picked grapefruit, abundant and weighty, from nearby trees. Always conscious of being a good host, Mr. Heifetz observed and participated like a host even if the location did not happen to be his own home. Wherever the occasion took place, there was a sense of old-worldliness because of his way of conducting the event.

At some of his parties there was dancing. He loved to dance, and, in my opinion, dancing with him exemplified his philosophy about performance. He often mentioned in class how important it was to present the music in such a way that people in the audience would be on the edge of their seats. This was true when he danced. I recall a New Year's Eve party where, playing the gracious host, he enjoyed asking the ladies for a dance. When it was my turn, I learned that he delighted in throwing me rhythmic and stylistic "curves," trying to see whether I would catch him in an unexpected move.

When the music ended, I thanked him hurriedly and was about to return to my seat when he said, "Just a minute. Where are you going? Come here!" And so we danced another dance with more of his tricky moves. He was a marvelous dancer, light on his feet and economical in his movements. I later learned that he had studied all dances, including the samba and rumba, with Mr. and Mrs. Arthur Murray. Yet another facet of his complexity—Jascha Heifetz, the ballroom dancer.

Among the most exciting of invitations to receive was the one to a Heifetz New Year's Eve party. There was always a spectacular list of planned activities, games, food, dancing and, of course, the music, live and recorded. Lusty and mysterious, soulful tunes of Zamfir, king of Romanian pan pipes, and the "all-over-the-keyboard" sounds of jazz pianist Erroll Garner enriched our hearts and souls. Other guests who had attended these festivities before my time included Jack Benny, Danny Kaye and the Ramos. Following the tradition in American homes across the nation, we tuned in to a New York station for the official countdown in Times Square. I loved these New Year's Eve gatherings, which were special memories in my life. When I was invited to the 1982 party, I recall, I decided to attend the party without a date. There was no one I particularly wanted to accompany me for the occasion. Ringing the bell with violin in hand and semi-formally dressed for the party, I took a deep breath. As I was ushered into Mr. Heifetz's home unaccompanied, my heart raced because of the fact that I was defying my teacher's specific request to bring a date. After combing my hair and applying some fresh lipstick, I walked into the sitting room just off the dining room. Mr. Heifetz, dressed in a white dinner jacket, welcomed me with a warm, glowing smile and said, "Charming! Charming!" as he looked around and behind me. "Where's your date?" he asked with a look of innocent wonder.

"I don't have a date, Mr. Heifetz," I said calmly.

He was shocked by what he considered to be my audacity. His parties were as carefully planned as his lessons, including the number of places that would be set for the guests. I was upsetting his plan, and he clearly regarded my decision to come alone as a form of defiance.

"But I told you to bring a date, didn't I?"

"Yes, you did, Mr. Heifetz," I replied. His big eyes met my equally big eyes. There was a long silence, and then I quietly said, "Mr. Heifetz, if I bring a date, you see, I have to go home with him . . . and there's no one with whom I want to do that." (I always suspected that my teacher believed me to lead a much more racy life than I really did. I recall a time after some of the first lessons in class when Mr. Heifetz's secretary Ann Neblett met me in the ladies' room and said, "Mr. H. just hopes that you won't get any diseases." I almost fainted! Just what did Mr. H. imagine that I did with my time? Perhaps my "trademark" huge dark circles under my eyes were a result of a very active social life? "Social" life based on …WHAT? My expressive music? My quiet, but knowing nature? My appearance?)

There was a look of recognition in his eyes. He understood what I was saying, but he remained distant toward me the entire evening.

Music making at Heifetz celebrations was always the high point. No matter where the party—Beverly Hills, Malibu, Palm Springs—there was always the anticipation of joining together in the creation of music. We never knew what music would be played. With Mr. Heifetz there was always the element of surprise. I might be asked to play first violin in a Haydn string quartet or the viola in a Mozart duo. But no matter what the repertoire or the instruments being played, the moment at which Mr. Heifetz joined in was a moment when life stood still for me. His magic never failed.

On New Year's Eve at his Beverly Hills home we played chamber music in the living room, a wonderfully comfortable place marked by many indelible Heifetz touches. To enter the sunken room, which had been converted from a porch, there was a small step down. Then immediately to the left was a lovely, small Steinway grand piano and to the rear of the piano a sitting area with a couch, a coffee table and a couple of chairs to either side. This space had a direct view of the fireplace, which had bookcases on either side of it. On a shelf at eye level sat a 75-inch model of his sloop, the 75-foot Serenade, which he and his first wife, Florence Vidor, owned and sailed while living in Newport Beach, California. To the right of the fireplace was a radio and a collection of LPs, but no cassette or CD players. The entire length of the room across from the entrance had sliding doors that could be moved aside to reveal a view of the Los Angeles skyline, and the roof of the room opened to a view of the stars. On a clear night the setting was exquisite.

Some of the repertoire that I remember playing over the years at these celebrations included the Beethoven *Piano Trio #1* with Leonard Pennario at the piano, *The Archduke Piano Trio*, the Beethoven *String Trios*, the Dohnanyi *Piano Quartet*, several Fritz Kreisler pieces, Haydn *String Quartets*, the Faure *String Quartet*, Schubert's *Trout Quintet*, the Tchaikovsky and Brahms *Sextets*, the Beethoven *Septet*, and the two Mozart *Viola Quintets*.

What exciting occasions these were! Music was the perfect vehicle to express gratitude for the old year and joy for the arrival of the new. An invitation to these New Year's Eve parties was a treasured prize.

*My mother wanted me to be the famous violinist Jascha Heifetz—only I couldn't because Jascha Heifetz was already Jascha Heifetz.*

*Once, he and I were on* The Ed Sullivan Show, *and afterward I took his violin by mistake. It was a Stradivarius, worth big, big dollars—and all the police were out looking for me. That's the closest I ever came to being Jascha Heifetz. I still play the violin—badly—in all my shows. It's a great prop.*
—Henny Youngman

# Final Understanding

"Live and sometimes learn."

Over the years I cherished Jascha Heifetz's visits and all the moments we spent making music together. Whether it was in class or at my apartment at the Knight piano he had given me, or on those celebratory occasions at his homes, music was the heartbeat of all those moments.

Shortly before he died I had a brief visit with him. I had moved to Oregon and was grateful for the opportunity to see him alone and to tell him just how great an impact he had made on my life. I said, "You know, Mr. Heifetz, every time I take out my violin and every time I teach a lesson, I realize just how much you have given to me. Thank you."

After a long, long silence, during which he seemed to be considering my words, he looked at me with those penetrating eyes for the last time. With that knowing look I had felt so many times over the years, he gently said, "Good!" His voice was filled with an expressiveness that I understood.

After his death I learned from an article that appeared in the *Los Angeles Times* that he had willed me his Carlo Tononi violin and one of his "four good bows." He had never discussed with me his desire that I become heiress to these treasures. Besides these gifts, I thought, he has left me with the greatest of all his surprises—the legacy of the master.

# Coda

"The concert will go on
whether I am there or not."
—when asked whether Mr. Heifetz would be coming
to hear a performance of a well-known violinist.

The Heifetz Master Class was a collection of a chosen few who have gone on to become representatives of a legacy that will live forever. It was a special class because Jascha Heifetz, the greatest violinist of them all, recognized his responsibility to provide an endowment for succeeding generations. He was teaching for all the right reasons, and his devotion to his students was a gift to us. Every day of my life I grow increasingly aware, as I live my own personal commitment to excellence, that the memory of my association with Mr. Heifetz enriches not only my life, but also the lives of all my hundreds of students and audiences.

In April of 1999 the Teaching Studio of Jascha Heifetz was formally dedicated in its new home at The Colburn School of Music in Los Angeles. Asked to perform one of the unpublished Heifetz transcriptions for the program, I waited backstage for my call. What moments I spent! I heard Mr. Heifetz's recorded voice and then heard his unbelievable and undeniable greatness as he performed on old videos. How could I step on stage with such powerful sounds of his presence echoing around me? Was I "ready" to play a work which I planned to dedicate with reverence to our teacher on behalf of all those to whom he had tirelessly devoted himself?

I don't remember much about my performance except that as I walked offstage into my dressing room, tears flooded my face. "Why me?" I asked myself. With all who entered his teaching world, why did he will me his beloved Tononi, the gift from his father? It had been years since I had lived that vastly rich experience with Jascha Heifetz, and now, being reunited in his space with his voice and his music, the tremendous magnitude of his gesture toward me—just *one* among the many who had sought him out—once more struck me numb. I became entranced. I saw his face with his all-knowing eyes, and he was smiling at me.

I suddenly understood:

He *knew* that I would do the right thing. It was that silent understanding we seemed to have from the beginning. The gesture of his gift to me was the ultimate, final display of confidence and respect one human being can show to another. And now, once again, in yet another eloquent moment of communication, came his message:

"Sherry, you *are* ready."

# Wit and Wisdom of Jascha Heifetz

Mr. Heifetz referred to the special little character pieces as "itsy-bitsies". Though most of this music was composed one hundred years ago, the charm, humor and emotion contained within deserves to be remembered.

Some of my favorite Mr. Heifetz "isty-bitsies" which reveal his personal charm and his sense of humor are included here.

### His advice on performing

"Keep your eyes on what you're doing, or you may have an accident." *Advising players who had roaming or closed eyes as they played.*

"You have to be convinced that whatever you are playing is the greatest piece in the world."

"It's good to be a little nervous before a concert, but if you are too nervous, get off the stage." *Responding to a student who expressed trepidation about stage fright.*

"It's not the error. It's the recovery that matters." *Referring to a breakdown during performance.*

"A concert should be on the short, not long side. Make the audience want more, not less."

"Keep the audience on the edge of their seats, not knowing what to expect."

"In sections which repeat (Bach, in particular), always do it differently. Never play the same."

"Do the repeats in the concert; that way, you have two chances at it!"

"Play the Paganini *Caprices* with piano accompaniment."

"Sonatas should be memorized."

"If a string breaks during a performance and you are closer to the end of the movement than to the middle of it, continue playing high up on another string, finish, walk off stage, change it, and continue with the next movement."

"Do what you want within the beat, but BE THERE for the next beat."

"Do it with dash. Then if you miss it, you miss it with dash."

"This is only the first movement. There is more to come, so SAVE it!" *Advising a student on a performance of Glazounov.*

"You look like you are digging potatoes! Put your fiddle up, plant your feet, and PLAY!"

"Don't YOU get excited. You must excite ME, the listener."

"Let's hear the beginning and the end . . . the middle happens." *His advice to me in class before I was to leave town for a concerto performance.*

"You might get applause, God forbid!" *Cautioning a player not to pause too long between phrases.*

"You must play with all your might when playing with a full orchestra." *His way of reminding a student that there's a lot more competition when so many other instruments are on stage.*

"With a little bit more excitement!"

"You need to choose your program." *Indicating that I must present my own musical strengths for a upcoming performance.*

### His responses to student classroom performance

"Good morning, one and all." *His class opener.*
"All right, boys and girls, LUNCH!" *After the morning session.*
"Ladies and gentlemen, CLASS DISMISSED!" *To end the day.*

"You always get another chance . . . that is, if you deserve it."

"Utilize, don't analyze."

"You have to know the rules before you can break them." *Referring to performance of Bach* Unaccompanied Sonatas and Partitas *with improvised rhythm.*

"Anything I should know?" *Asked of me, his assistant, before inviting students into the classroom.*

"Sounds like a neurotic trill." *A wild vibrato sound lacking a fast individual finger placement.*

"Don't slide into the base. This is NOT baseball."
"Just hit it!"

"You play like a horse running back into the barn."

"You may be ready for Beethoven. But he is not ready for you."

"It sounds very UN-exciting."

"Do you have any other interests?" *Acerbic remark after a dull performance by a student.*

"Hold it!" *Bellowed at any student who continued to play when he wished to comment.*

"Take out the glissando. You don't feel it."

"Ah, do you think you could control your hysterics in this movement?" *Responding to a student performance of the slow movement of the Tchaikovsky* Violin Concerto.

"Too, too, too, TOO many." *Referring to the use of slides.*

"This classroom has a two-way door." *Indicating that a student's future in the class was in jeopardy.*

"Hello, hello, hello!" *His way of calling attention to a special situation.*

"Live and sometimes learn."

"Don't play all the notes, just more or less." *To the pianist in regard to a piano reduction of an orchestral score.*

"Write it down." *Suggestion offered as a way to remember items to be dealt with.*

"You look as if you might take a leap." *When a performer changed stance from side to side.*

"Well, it would be nice if we finished together!"

"Don't be scared. I won't play." *As he tuned his violin.*

"MAKE a fuss over it." *Directing a student to emphasize an F sharp minor harmony.*

"Do it! You're in the mood. Just do it!"

"You could learn to like it . . . it's a nice one." *(Bach Sonata)*

"Which one [of the Paganini *Caprices*] have you prepared?"
*Student response:* "None of them."
*Heifetz response:* "Good. Play #17."

"I should commend you for bravery." *When a student chose to play scales in class.*

"You're still in one piece." *After the student played the scales.*

"More pep . . . you're at the END . . . so GET it."

"Do it any way you want as long as it comes out."

"You have no toni." *no tone—a play on words 'Tononi violin'*

*"Don't practice mistakes."*

**His reaction to some people and things that annoyed him**

"Hocus pocus." *His name for the suggestions and so-called remedies of people he considered to be "do-gooders."*

"Calamity Janes." *The high drama types who ALWAYS seem to be caught in a dilemma and ALWAYS have an excuse.*

"Pipe down!" *His admonition to noisy blue jays, loud speaking voices, loud pianists, and loud cellists in chamber music.*

"I ran out of medals." *Responding to those who tried desperately to impress him.*

"Music is not athletics." *Explaining why he was unable to endorse musical competitions.*

"How can I help someone who is already in a professional position?" *After receiving an application from a member of the Boston Symphony.*

"I don't want to year Ysaye in auditions; they are all over the place." *Referring to the tendency of players to totally improvise the rhythm in the pieces.*

"Why would you want to go to a competition? Who will be judging you? And what are THEIR qualifications?"

"What's funnier than people?"

"There are already enough of those sorts of things (ceramics) in this world." *After learning that I was enrolled in a ceramics class.*

"When I sell this house, I WILL have a picture taken." *Responding to a well known violinist fan at the beach who wanted to take a photo of Mr. Heifetz in his surroundings.*

"So many things have already been done. Let them put together material that already exists." *Responding to a request from Charles Kuralt for an interview for* CBS Sunday Morning *in the early 1980's.*

### His observations on himself

"The concert will go on whether I am there or not." *When asked by a well-known violinist visiting class whether Mr. H. would be attending his performance with the Los Angeles Philharmonic.*

"I am not ready, but I am not getting any readier." *Answering as to his readiness at a recording session.*

"If I don't practice one day, I know it; two days, the critics know it; three days, the public knows it." *Quoted in* SanFrancisco Examiner *and* Chronicle, *18 April, 1971.*

"I occasionally play works by contemporary composers for two reasons. First, to discourage the composer from writing any more, and second, to remind myself how much I appreciate Beethoven." *Quoted in LIFE magazine, 28 July, 1961.*

"Ketch me if you can." *To the pianist in class as he jumped into the middle of a work in demonstration.*

"First, I am going to play you something you may not like,

but it's GOOD FOR YOU . . . like spinach." *Before playing a Bach Partita for several GI's sitting on the ground a mile or two behind the front lines west of the Rhine in the fall of 1944.*

"I can't get involved in politics." *Responding to my explanation that a Chinese student had had to work in the rice fields during the Cultural Revolution and had not been permitted to play the violin during those years.*

"Sherry, I CAN'T do it." *Regarding pressure he was receiving to participate in a publicity campaign to heighten visibility of his class.*

## His occasional observations about me
*(These personal comments directed toward me are a reflection on the kinds of comments he made to students in his class, his way of expressing concern for each of us.)*

"Sherry Netherlands." *Pet name for me inspired by a prestigious New York hotel.*

"Fairy Princess, are you of this world or some other world?" *Referring to me following a Halloween costume party.*

"Are you with us?" *An appropriate jab at my tendency to "disappear" from the moment.*

"A fetching coat." *Referring to my red, mid-length velvet coat with a shawl collar, a relic of the 1950's, worn to class one day.*

"You will make it but will probably have to come in through the back door." *After my signing with Harold Shaw management.*

"Isn't there anything else you can do?" *Following my return from New York management and recording company talks.*

"You know, Sherry, one day you may decide to get married. YOU HAVE GOT TO DO SOMETHING ABOUT YOUR COOKING!"

"What would you do if you couldn't play the violin?" *A question he asked of me at my first audition with him.*

"Nya, nya, nya. You play everything like a love song."

"You'll probably do better without me." *After learning that I was leaving to perform the Mendelssohn Concerto without his having heard it.*

"She has some very lovely qualities . . . one might even say Sherry is adorable." *To guests at his home in my embarrassed presence.*

"Why does she do that? Why doesn't she tell me?" *Referring to my quiet way of doing things, such as bringing a special token of thanks to his home and leaving it in the kitchen to be discovered later, or making a recording, or playing a broadcast without telling him.*

"You know what you have to do. Get an unlisted number!" *Following threatening phone calls which I had received.*

"He's not for you." *Message delivered to me via his secretary regarding the date I had brought to a New Year's Eve gathering.*

"She likes sweets. Give her some of Cookie's cookies!" *Offering me treats from his niece Cookie, who lived in New York. The cookies, which he treasured, were special powdered sugar butter confections for the holidays.*

"Don't you EAT at home? You are too thin. Give her a second helping."

"We have to do something about that car!" *Regarding my yellow Fiat, which he called my lemon, and not just because of its color.* "Does it have good brakes and tires?"

"Anyone follow you?" *A remark inspired by my adventures which he considered outlandish.*

"Maybe Sherry can use these." *Linen napkins from his home passed on to me after he had visited my bare little garage apartment.*

"You don't have to run around the world to play . . . I traveled enough for you, too."

### His advice on grooming

"I see we have a new member in class today . . . Jack, would you like to play?" *After our class member, Jacqueline, appeared in class with a chic, new short hair style.*

"Lubricate it." *Referring to the area on a violinist's neck that experiences abrasions from the chin rest and* "keep it clean." *Referring to the chin rest.*

"Do I know you?" *To a student with a new hair-do.*

"Your barber is looking for you." *Gentle reminder to remain well-groomed for class.*

"Your merry board is your best friend." *referring to the use of an emery board for finger calluses.*

"What do you do? Get dressed in the dark?"

"Wouldn't you say that Sherry's skirt is a 'Yiddle-bit' short?"

"See my doctor." *After he noticed an unattractive mole on my neck at the beach.*

"Just WHAT are you wearing?" *Displeased with the culottes I wore to class.* "Those are pants."

## Some miscellaneous remarks

"Honk two times." *When driving an automobile around a blind corner.*

"The pleasure and perils of travel!"

"Down the hatch!" *Signaling guests to gulp down vodka in unison following a toast.*

"Is it a 'moveable feast?'" *An allusion used many times by Mr. H. before I learned he was referring to a favorite book of his by Ernest Hemingway.*

"Just good old-fashioned spit on a cloth." *When asked what he used to clean his violin strings.*

"You are very lucky in life if you can count on two friends." *Counting off on two fingers of his hand.*

"Do you know any yokes (jokes)?"

"There are always three points of view: his hers, and the truth."

~

Perhaps his most haunting and prophetic words which I remember, occurred during a game of ping-pong at Malibu. Seemingly out of nowhere, with a sense of inevitability, he said to me:

**"You'll write the book."**

~

# Itsy-Bitsy *

### by Sherry Kloss ♪

♪ *Eulogy delivered on Jefferson Public radio, Ashland Oregon, the day of Mr. Heifetz's passing.*

I will always remember . . .

You opened the gates to the beyond and filled our hearts with beauty.

You inspired generations to quality and shared your most personal beliefs for excellence.

You showed us how to capture a wide range of emotions in just mere few moments WITHOUT UTTERING A WORD . . . ILLUMINATING THE TRUE MEANING OF EXISTENCE.

This world forever will bear the testimony of your loving devotion.

I will always remember . . .

---

* A term used by Mr. Heifetz to denote a short piece

## Rudyard Kipling's Verse

### IF—
"BROTHER SQUARE-TOES"—REWARDS AND FAIRIES

IF YOU can keep your head when all about you
    Are losing theirs and blaming it on you,
If you can trust yourself when all men doubt you,
    But make allowance for their doubting too;
If you can wait and not be tired by waiting,
    Or being lied about, don't deal in lies,
Or being hated, don't give way to hating,
    And yet don't look too good, nor talk too wise:

If you can dream—and not make dreams your master,
    If you can think—and not make thoughts your aim;
If you can meet with Triumph and Disaster
    And treat those two impostors just the same;
If you can bear to hear the truth you've spoken
    Twisted by knaves to make a trap for fools,
Or watch the things you gave your life to, broken,
    And stoop and build 'em up with worn out tools:

If you can make one heap of all your winnings
    And risk it on one turn of pitch-and-toss,
And lose, and start again at your beginnings
    And never breathe a word about your loss;
If you can force your heart and nerve and sinew
    To serve your turn long after they are gone,
And so hold on when there is nothing in you
    Except the Will which says to them: "Hold on!"

If you can talk with crowds and keep your virtue,
    Or walk with Kings—nor lose the common touch,
If neither foes nor loving friends can hurt you,
    If all men count with you, but none too much;
If you can fill the unforgiving minute
    With sixty seconds' worth of distance run,
Yours is the Earth and everything that's in it,
    And—which is more—you'll be a Man, my son!

# Words to Live By

### By Jascha Heifetz

**"If you can meet with Triumph and Disaster
And treat those two impostors just the same..."**

It's not the thing to quote Kipling's "If" any more, I am told. But the poem was popular when I made my debut in this country. I learned it by heart then, took it to heart then, and have carried it about with me since.

Perhaps the words mean something special to me–because an artist, whose life is in the public eye, must steer a mean course between triumph and disaster and learn to live with both. In many ways triumph is the greater test. Many a man who emerges a hero under suffering succumbs to success. I met triumph early–at seven years–and never had to face disaster until quite grown up. My first severe criticism was a terrible shock to me and a hard lesson. But even harder for one's artistic balance is the heady wine of continuous praise. Yes, triumph and disaster go hand-in-hand with a career. They are the two faces of the coin which is the currency of the world of art.

O.K.–J.H.

# The Heifetz Caprices
## Photo Album

Photo credit: BMG Classics

# Class

Chamber music with Jeffrey Solow, cello & Ayke Agus, piano.
Yukiko Kamai and Sherry Kloss assist.

Creating a special moment in the music with Yukiko Kamai.
Tony Sen, background.

Encouraging more intensity in the music, with Sherry Kloss, violin & Ayke Agus, piano. Barbara Nortd observes.

Demonstrating a musical point to Christiaan Borr.

The Heifetz Caprices 133

Benjamin Rosen, proprietor of Globe Music.

In protest of Los Angeles smog with students
Robert Witte, Varujan Kodjian, Claire Hodgkins, Ellen Mack,
Adam Han-Gorske near Clark House at USC.

Sherry Kloss at side gate of Heifetz home ringing bell to the studio at precisely 11:00 a.m. for class.

# The Social Gatherings

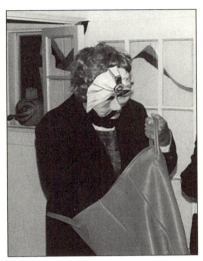

J.H. arrives at Halloween party with L.L Bean bag full of surprises.

Greeting other costumed guests Marilyn Summers and Ayke Agus with jack-in-the-box in his hand.

Be-wigged and in his glory with Rudolph Kulman, background.

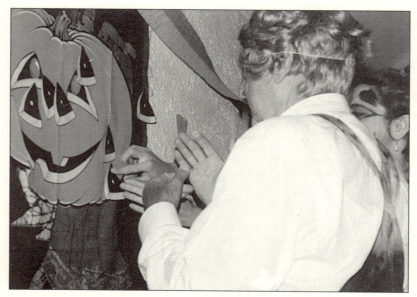

Blind-folded and playing pin the nose on the pumpkin.

## The Heifetz Caprices

Claire Hodgkins, Christiaan Borr.

Rudiger Liebermann.

Rudiger bobbing for apples, Robert Summers, S.K., background.

Opening a Halloween token from
Jacqueline Brand: "Is it safe?"

"Fairy princess" S.K.

Sherry has just blown out the candles on her birthday cake;
Tony Sen and J.H. remove the candles and join in the celebration.

What a tone!

The mechanical clown bank used in class. A coin was placed
in the hand of the clown, when lever was depressed,
the hand fed the mouth, and the eyes fluttered.

# The Beach

Enjoying discussion at lunch with Yukiko and Ayke.

S.K. tends to her job as "fire captain" for the day.

With Jack Pfeiffer, longtime colleague and friend.

Ping-pong doubles with partner S.K.,
Ayke Agus & Soo Young Yoon in tea house.

# The Heifetz Caprices 143

Students Mark Giannini, Sando Xia & Soo Young Yoon
in tea house overlooking the Pacific Ocean.

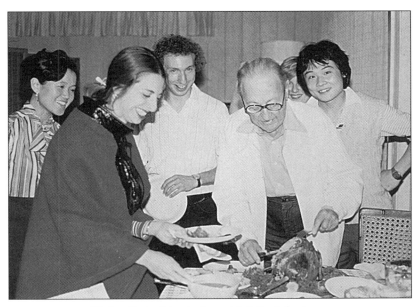

Slicing the holiday turkey with S.K., Ayke Agus,
Elliot Markow, Maarit Kirvessalo & Yuki Mori.

Class Portrait; 1st row: Maarit Kirvessalo, Elliot Markow, J.H. & S.K. 2nd row: Sando Xia, Ayke Agus, Yuki Mori.

With Muriel Moebius & S.K. Asked to move closer for this photo, J.H. replied "but I don't really know them well enough." Prodded again, he pulled us close and laughed saying, "Well, now I do."

# The Heifetz Caprices

S.K. and Ayke Agus in tea house (near one of the posts which Sherry smashed during the game of Pinÿata), wearing international hats from the house.

S.K. blindfolds Yukiko Kamai while J.H. secures her hat in preparation for her turn at the game of Pinÿata.

J.H. spins blind-folded Yukiko around 3 times before "sending" her off bat in hand, during a game of Pinÿata.

J.H. accepts "gift-wrapped" wheel barrow of oak and pine.
Mary Lou Burns, Secretary, Ayke Agus, Ann Tremaine

# New Year's
(Beverly Hills)

S.K. & J.H.

With Ayke Agus, piano, Ann Tremaine,
Siok Lie Agus, page turner.

Affectionate pat for S.K. mid-performance.

With S.K., background Ann Tremaine.

With long-time dear friend Tamara Chapro
in joyful celebration (Malibu).

# Other Materials

J.H. visits class taught by Claire Hodgkins,
at Loma Linda University.

J.H. with several G.I.s a mile or two behind the front lines west of the
Rhine in the fall of 1944. *From the collection of Joseph Gold.*

J.H. with friends, 1911.

The Heifetz Caprices 153

Programs from his 1921 Australian Tour

Direction................J. & N. Tait

*Programme*

**FIRST CONCERT**

1.
Chaconne ............................... *Vitali*
(Arranged by Charlier)

2.
Concerto in E Minor, Op. 64 ............. *Mendelssohn*
　Allegro Molto Appassionato.
　Andante.
　Allegretto Non Troppo: Allegretto Molto Vivace.

3.
(a) Ave Maria ......................... Schubert
(b) Menuet ............................ Mozart
(c) Nocturne in D. Major ................ Chopin
(d) Perpetuum Mobile .................... Ries

4.
Melodie ............................ Tschaikovsky
Ronde des Lutins........................ Bazzini

At the Piano
**ISIDOR ACHRON**
*"His Master's Voice" Records.*

Programs from his 1921 Australian Tour

J.H. photographed by Falk in 1924 with the Tononi violin.
*Autographed:* Sincerely, Jascha Heifetz, Los Angeles, 1924

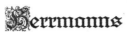 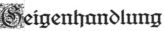

Emil Herrmann
Berlin W62 ❖ Bayreutherstraße 30

Unterzeichneter garantiert hiermit, dass die heute an Herrn R. Heifetz, Violin Virtuose, zur Zeit Dresden.Loschwitz, Kurhaus Rochwitz, verkaufte Violine mit dem Zettel: "Carlo Tononi Bolognese fece in Venezia l'A: 1736" von diesem Meister gemacht wurde.

Beschreibung: Der Boden ist geteilt. Der Lack ist rotbraun.

Die Länge des Bodens beträgt 35,4 cm.
Die obere Breite des Bodens beträgt 16,7 cm.
Die untere Breite des Bodens beträgt 20,4 cm.

Reparaturen, die im Laufe der Zeit an dem Instrumente durch Gebrauch und Abnützung nötig wurden, sind von der Garantie für die Originalität genannter Meister ausgeschlossen.

den 3. August 1914

Emil Herrmann

Translation:   Herrmanns Violin Dealers
Emil Herrmann
Berlin W62, Bayreutherstrasse 30
CERTIFICATE

The undersigned guarantees hereby that the violin sold today to Mr. R. Heifetz, Violin Virtuoso, presently in Dresden, Loschwitz, Kurhaus Rochwitz, bearing the label: "Carlo Tononi Bolognese fece in Venezia l'A: 1736" is the work of this master.
DESCRIPTION: The back is of two pieces. The varnish is red-brown.
The length of the base is: 35.4 cm.
The upper width of the back is: 16.7 cm.
The lower width of the back is: 20.4 cm.
Repairs to the instrument which were necessary in the course of time because of use and wear and tear are not included in the guarantee as being the original work of the named master.

This 3rd of August, 1914
Emil Herrmann

1520 GILCREST DRIVE
BEVERLY HILLS, CALIFORNIA

May, 1979

    SHERRY KLOSS is attending (from time to time) my class at U.S.C. as a teacher and auditor.

    She is a fine concert <u>violinist</u> and is a patient and understanding <u>teacher</u>.

    I recommend her most heartily for either-- and as a charming Person she has all my best wishes.

*Jascha Heifetz*

1520 GILCREST DRIVE
BEVERLY HILLS, CALIFORNIA

Oct. 31, 1980

6. To <u>Sherry Kloss</u> my Tononi Violin, and one of my 4 good bows — if she does not survive me — then to my Estate.

Jascha Heifetz

Photo: Janae Polish

# The Jascha Heifetz Transcriptions
### Sherry Kloss, violin
### Zeyda Ruga Suzuki, piano

Presented by the fifth quadrennial
International Violin Competition of Indianapolis
as part of the
International Forum on Violins

September 16, 1998, 2:00 p.m.
Christel DeHaan Fine Arts Center
University of Indianapolis

February 24, 1989

Ms Sherry Kloss
55 Pompadour Drive
Ashland, Oregon 97520

Dear Sherry:

Please forgive my long delay in thanking you for the wonderful picture of JH and me. I had misplaced it and I have reached the age when if something isn't staring at me daily, I tend to forget it! But it's safe and sound, and it's indeed a precious remembrance. There are so many, and I cherish them all.

I've heard your Protone Record, and I think it's a sheer delight. I think Jim would have liked it, too.

I hope everything is going well for you. I'm fine and still full of beans and hope to stay that way for a long time. Thank you again for the wonderful picture. Stay well and be happy.

With warmest wishes,

Sincerely yours,

Love, Jack

John F. Pfeiffer
Executive Producer
Red Seal Artists and Repertoire

JFP/ms

# The Heifetz Caprices

```
                    PROGRAM
              SHERRY KLOSS - VIOLINIST
              AYKE AGUS  — PIANIST
                         I
SONATA No.(g minor)                    G. TARTINI
  Andante
  Non troppo presto
  Largo: Allegro comodo

SONATA (for VIOLIN and PIANO 1949)     G. BEGLARIAN
  Moderato
  Adagio
  Allegro scherzando
                         II
SONATA (in Eb MAJOR)                   BEETHOVEN
  Allegro con spirito
  Adagio con molt' espressione
  Rondo: Allegro molto
                         III
Preludio (from Partita III)            J.S. BACH - J. HEIFETZ
CAPRICE No. 14                         PAGANINI

                         IV
Dance Espagnole                        de Falla - Kreisler
  from "La Vida Breve"   b.
Nocturne,                 a.           Chopin - Sarasate
Polonaise Brillante       c.           Wieniawski
        (2 pieces)
```

Mr. Heifetz's comments on programming.

*Too short*  ②

Duo for Violin & Piano — Schubert

Fantasy for Harp & Violin — Saint Saens
2 Caprices — Paganini
Zephir *spelling!?* — Hubay

? Caprice Basque — Sarasate
Polonaise in D Major — (Wieniawski) *spelling*

Sherry Kloss

# The Heifetz Caprices

## Wigmore Hall
Manager: William Lyne
Lessees: Arts Council

### Friday 28 February 1986 at 7.30pm

# SHERRY KLOSS
*violin*

# GERALD ROBBINS
*piano*

Sonatas by Beethoven (Kreutzer)
Mozart, Howard Ferguson, Franck

# Sherry Kloss

Among the foremost violinists of her generation, Sherry Kloss has performed to great acclaim throughout the United States, Canada, Europe and Australia. Her "singing style" reflects the influence of her close association as pupil and master-teaching assistant to Jascha Heifetz. Her recordings, "Forgotten Gems" and "Lost & Found Treasures of the Heifetz Legacy" have received national recognition with extensive interviews on NPR's "Weekend Edition", "Performance Today", and "The Studs Terkel Almanac." She holds the prestigious Honorary Degree of Excellence from Siena, Italy's Academia Chigiana Musicale and serves as adjudicator for International competitions. In 1998, Pittsburgh, Pennsylvania issued a proclamation recognizing Sherry Kloss as a prominent Pittsburgh artist. She is the Founder and Artistic Director of the "Music Institute for the Development of Personal Style" at Southern Oregon University, and Co-founder of "Jascha Heifetz Society." Professor of Violin and Sursa Distinguished Professor in Fine Arts at Ball State University, Muncie, Indiana, Miss Kloss plays the Heifetz-Tononi violin willed to her by Jascha Heifetz. In addition to music, she is passionate about the outdoors, swimming and the Argentine Tango.

Photo: Janae Polish

A portion of the proceeds from this publication will benefit the scholarship fund for the Music Institute for the Development of Personal Style and Jascha Heifetz Society.

Special thanks to Richard O. Price, retired English teacher and department chairperson at Carrick High School in Pittsburgh, Pennsylvania, my high school English teacher, whose guidance, enthusiasm, and expertise brought this book to its fruition.